Bedroom
Feng Shui

Bedroom Feng Shui

REVISED EDITION

CLEAR ENGLEBERT

iUniverse, Inc.
Bloomington

BEDROOM FENG SHUI
REVISED EDITION

iUniverse books may be ordered through booksellers or by contacting:

iUniverse
1663 Liberty Drive
Bloomington, IN 47403
www.iuniverse.com
1-800-Authors (1-800-288-4677)

ISBN: 978-1-4620-5155-7 (sc)
ISBN: 978-1-4620-5154-0 (ebk)

First edition originally published in 2001 by The Crossing Press
Front and back cover design by Rick Mears
Photography, including cover, by Steve Mann
Drawings by Steve Mann and Rick Mears
The cover bed is courtesy of Alysee and Larry Catron
The bed on page 26 provided by CS Wo & Son / Furnitureland

Printed in the United States of America

iUniverse rev. date: 10/19/2011

CONTENTS

Preface

The first edition of *Bedroom Feng Shui* was published in 2001 by The Crossing Press. I'm writing this preface to the second edition ten years later, and I've seen many more homes and learned much more in that time. This new edition is significantly expanded and improved.

One of the things that has remained extremely important in my practice is that the feng shui solutions be appropriate to the person's style and taste—not *my* style and taste—*your* style and taste. I'd prefer that you use the things you already own, instead of buying new things. Some things are so commonly used that they have become associated with feng shui—crystals and mirrors, for instance. But almost anything can be a feng shui tool, if it is used skillfully.

The other thing that I emphasize is—no superstition. I give reasons and rationale for all the problems and solutions that I mention. I don't believe in "lucky objects." I believe in powerful symbolism.

Chapter 1

The Importance of the Bedroom in Feng Shui

What is Feng Shui?

The words are pronounced fung shway, and they mean *wind/water*. Feng shui is the Chinese art of placement. It originated in the mountains of China between three and five thousand years ago. It is popular because it works. Feng shui offers a system of arranging furniture and objects to assist you in accomplishing your goals and reaching your highest potential.

The old Taoist masters of China greatly respected nature. It was their teacher, and there is no end to learning from nature. All of nature and the movement of wind and water are considered to be an expression of *chi* energy.

Chi Energy

Chi is the basic energy of the universe. The concept of chi energy is easy to grasp if you think of it as energy that gets your attention. A car with flashing lights and blaring siren attracts a lot of chi energy because it is extremely noticeable. Heads turn and energy is required to make those neck muscles move. This is one aspect of chi energy. A wind chime has the same effect. When people hear it, they often turn their heads.

Some of the things that attract chi energy most strongly are light, brilliant color, movement, sound, and stunning beauty. The advertisers of the world learned these lessons long ago.

That's why television commercials often attract your attention more than the program.

To understand how chi energy flows inside your home, be aware of what gets your attention first. For example, if the first thing you notice in a room is a clean, bubbly fish tank, that's good. It probably puts a smile on your face and makes your eyes light up. But if the first thing you notice is a window with a distant view, you may be smiling, but your attention is miles away. One of the goals of feng shui is to keep your attention gracefully flowing around a room. The chi should be sweetly meandering.

Your home has vibrant chi energy to the degree that it feels vibrant. If the first thing you notice in a room is how cluttered and full of furniture it is, then the chi energy is stagnant. A bedroom should feel restful. A multifunctional bedroom may have to be used during the day, but at night you should be able to change it easily into a restful mode.

As another way to consider how chi flows, think about how you are able to move within a space. For example, think about a long hall that allows you to move quickly, like a bullet from a gun barrel. The bullet is harmful, and so is the speeding chi energy. The ideal traffic pattern of energy in a room is gently curved; you should be able to reach all areas without having to cautiously step over or around objects.

Think of yourself as an example of chi energy—because that is what you are. How you feel within a space is a good indicator of how chi is flowing there.

Solutions

There are two kinds of solutions to feng shui problems: real and symbolic. A real solution actually fixes the problem and changes the situation. A symbolic solution is used when a real solution is not feasible. The symbolic solution is a physical symbol of how you wish the situation were. When using a symbolic solution, say your intention out loud at the moment that you are installing it. You are thereby strengthening it by expressing it. In my opinion you are speaking to your angels or guardian beings, who hear you but can't read your mind.

The Importance of the Bedroom

The bedroom is the most important room in the home according to feng shui. If you sleep eight hours per night, that's a third of twenty-four hours; therefore a third of your life is spent in that room. Most people spend more time in the bedroom than in any other room. The more time you spend in a particular room, the more influence that room has on your life. This applies even if you are asleep—the room is still affecting you.

Universal agreement is a rare thing in feng shui, and some feng shui authorities maintain that the kitchen is the most important room in the home, because the food that fuels a person's life is prepared there. But modern "conveniences" such as microwaves, dishwashers, and prepared foods mean that less time today is spent in food preparation, and people now eat in restaurants more often than in the past—some people literally never cook. Both rooms are important, but kitchens are not always as important as they were a hundred years ago.

People aren't all the same, and they never will be, but almost everyone sleeps in their bedroom. I've had only one feng shui client who ignored her nice bedroom and chose to sleep every night on the comfy couch in her living room. Some people do that on an occasional basis, but this woman did it every night. After she told me where she slept, I ceased emphasizing her bedroom, and re-evaluated her living room.

Chapter 2

Location of the Bedroom

Some parts of a home are better places for bedrooms than others. Even if you have no choice about the location of your bedroom, it is still important to know what factors may be affecting you due to its location. The first factor used in feng to evaluate the location of the bedroom is the concept of *yin/yang*.

Yin/Yang

Everything that exists is classified as primarily yin or yang. Nothing is totally yin or totally yang. Everything is on a scale—more yin or more yang.

YIN	YANG
Lower part of a room	Upper part of a room
Private	Public
Moist	Dry
Dark	Light
Many things	Few things
Complex	Simple
Feminine	Masculine
Cold	Hot
Soft	Hard
Quiet	Loud
Indoors	Outdoors
Stillness	Movement
Death	Life

Horizontal	Vertical
Sleep	Awake
Closed and Tight	Open and Expansive
Textured	Slick and Shiny

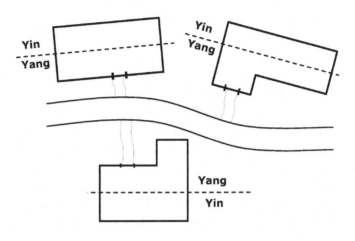

The yin & yang (front & rear) of a house

Fig. 2.1

Imagine the floor plan of your home, or draw it if that's more helpful. Then draw a line through it from side to side. The rear half of a home (based on the formal front door as the front) has a more relaxed energy than the front half. That energy is called *yin*. The front of a home has a more active, or *yang*, energy. You don't always have a choice about where your bedroom will be—but if you do, pick a room at the rear of the house. The energy there is conducive to deeper rest.

Occasionally the rear of the home is more active than the front, such as when a large highway is just beyond your back yard. The situation dictates how to apply the rules—in fact, one of the names of Form School feng shui is Situation School.

The front door of your home is referred to as the "mouth of chi." It partakes of an active energy even if a side door is more commonly used in everyday life. If your bedroom is in the front of the house or close to any street, I suggest a fairly heavy window treatment. Venetian blinds alone are a bit skimpy in this case. It would be better to have sheers in the daytime and heavy, sound-absorbing drapes (such as velvet) at night.

Another aspect of yin/yang concerns the size of the bedroom. The larger a room is the more yang it is. A small bedroom is cozy and nice and contains the quiet, restful energy well. The larger a bedroom is the more likely there will be restless sleep or worse—a troubled relationship. Extremely large bedrooms can be a factor in unfaithful relationships. The intimate energy of the partners is dissipated in the huge room. I've seen this repeatedly in my career. A canopy bed with curtains that actually close at night would help. An overly large bedroom can be made to seem smaller and cozier by using warmer and darker colors. No bedroom should ever be larger than the living room of the house. If so, the energy of the house is severely disturbed. An alcove can be added to a bedroom to make it feel larger, but the alcove should feel like a separate space. This can be done with curtains dividing the alcove from the bedroom proper.

Small bedrooms are just fine. Using light colors makes them even better.

Bedrooms Extending Beyond the Bulk of the House

If a bedroom protrudes beyond the bulk of the house it can have a feeling of separateness. If you sleep there you may not feel as connected to the rest of the household as you would in a bedroom located within the main shape of the house. (This is of special concern with children's rooms.) In this case, a mirror is used on the wall of the bedroom that connects to the main body of the house. The mirror should face into the bedroom. If putting a mirror on that bedroom wall is not an option, then look to Fig. 2.2 for examples of other walls in the home that should have a mirror. Only one wall needs a mirror—whichever one works best in your situation.

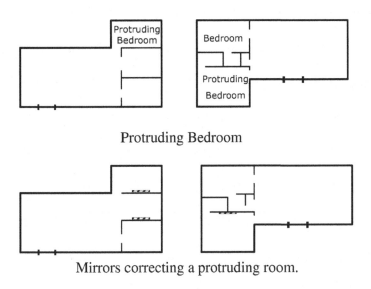

Protruding Bedroom

Mirrors correcting a protruding room.

Fig. 2.2

Mirrors can simulate the effect of a window. When you are looking into that window, the extending bedroom is seen within the main part of that house. The mirror symbolically pulls the bedroom into the main body of the house. The mirrors in the illustration would reflect the bedroom if some of the walls were gone. The walls do not have to disappear to serve the feng shui purpose.

An L-shaped house is said to have a meat cleaver shape. One wall is the "sharp blade" wall and is not auspicious. To find the blade wall, make a drawing of the outside walls of your house as if you were looking down on it. Locate the longest continuous outside wall—then look for the parallel wall on the other side of the house which is *farthest from* the longest wall. That's the blade wall. To sleep with the head of your bed at the blade wall is considered to be bad for your health (among other things). Don't spend a lot of time at that wall—don't have a lounge chair, couch, or desk chair there. If the head of the bed (or any of the three seating pieces just mentioned) must be against that wall, put a mirror on the opposite side of the room, facing into the room. The mirror symbolically moves the furniture (and person) to the other wall. See Fig. 2.3. Usually mirrors at the foot of the bed are not recommended in feng shui—this is an exception. When you place the mirror, say out loud something like, "This is to move the bed (or chair, etc.) onto this wall. It is no longer on the blade wall."

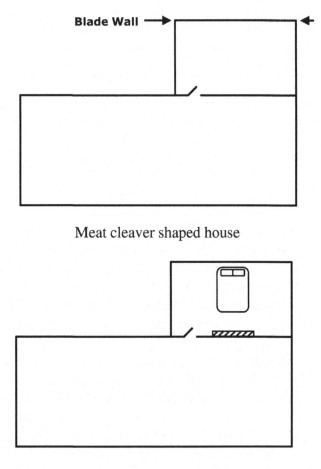

Meat cleaver shaped house

Mirror moving bed from blade wall

Fig. 2.3

Garages

If a bedroom is located directly above a garage, you may not be getting your best rest there. However, if cars are never parked in it, a garage is no problem for sleepers. Cars have very active come-and-go yang energy, and such a garage is too close to the place where sleep energy should be emphasized. To aid restful sleep in this situation you can put very heavy solid objects on the floor of the bedroom. Two examples would be a sculpture or a table supported by a marble base.

You can hang a crystal over the car in the garage. This can be done even if the garage door opens inward—use your ingenuity.

You can also put a mirror (any kind, any size) on the ceiling of the garage, reflecting the top of the car. Alternately, a very small mirror can be put under a rug or carpet in the bedroom, facing down toward the car.

As is often the case in feng shui, more is better. If possible do all three things, then do so. If a bedroom is directly behind a garage, there is a similar problem, because the "metal beast" is pointed directly at a sleep area and undue pressure could be felt in your life. Place a mirror on the back wall of the garage, so that it reflects the front of the car away from the bedroom. A reversed mirror could also be put in the bedroom with the reflective side pointing at the wall and at the car on the other side. A mirror in the garage is preferable to the reversed mirror in the bedroom. If you must face a mirror to the wall, cover it somehow so it doesn't look weird.

Kitchens

If a kitchen is located directly over a bedroom, a small mirror should be placed on the ceiling of the bedroom, reflecting up. The mirror symbolically reflects away and seals off the bustling kitchen vibrations from the quiet bedroom. The mirror can be quite small—even one inch will work. Such mirrors are available in craft and hobby stores. You can paint the back of the mirror the same color as the ceiling. Remember when using mirrors as a symbolic cure to always say out loud, at the moment you install the mirror, your purpose for placing the mirror. It could be a simple as, "This is to reflect away the energy on the other side, so that it doesn't affect the peaceful bedroom." You can also hang a crystal from the ceiling of the bedroom, with the intention of dispersing the influence of the kitchen that is above.

If a kitchen is directly below any part of a bedroom, there can be more restlessness in that bedroom. Put at least one very small mirror on the floor of the bedroom, with the reflective side pointed down. The mirror can be placed under rugs or furniture. Alternatively, you can place one or more mirrors on the ceiling of the kitchen (reflective side pointing down), and paint over the reflective side with the ceiling color. Also, a crystal can be hung from the kitchen ceiling, with the intention of dispersing the kitchen's influence before it gets absorbed into the bedroom above it.

A bedroom and a kitchen really shouldn't share a wall at all. If they must share a wall, put a mirror on that wall. The reflective side of the mirror should face the kitchen, which is seen to be a potential disturber of peaceful bedroom energy. The mirror can be in the bedroom and/or in the kitchen, as long as it is attached to the shared wall. Remember to say your intention: "To reflect away the yang energy of the kitchen."

No bedroom door should open directly into a kitchen, and it's even worse if the bedroom door directly faces the kitchen stove. It goes against common sense as well as feng shui. One room should be quiet and restful and one room is active with the bustle of food preparation. Hang a crystal between the stove and the door.

Microwave ovens almost always have high electromagnetic fields around them (including *behind* them) when they are on, from a distance (depending on the oven) of about four feet to almost 20 feet. Built-in microwave ovens usually have high EMF leakage—much more than counter-top models. A built-in microwave oven should not be directly behind the head of a bed, on the other side of the wall. If there is no other choice, do not turn the oven on when someone is in the bed. There's no microwave oven in my home, but I've measured thousands of them with a gaussmeter. Only the high-end Viking built-in microwave ovens seem to have very low EMF leakage. When any counter-top microwave is turned on, be sure to step back at least four feet, and this is especially important for children. More information on EMFs is in Chapter 7.

Sometimes the head of a bed must be located directly behind a refrigerator, on the other side of the wall. Most refrigerators don't have excessively high EMFs, but they do hum occasionally, so a symbolic cure is called for. Put a mirror between the bed and the refrigerator to reflect the electrical, buzzing refrigerator away from the quiet bed. The mirror can be in the kitchen or in the bedroom, with the reflective side toward the refrigerator.

Height of the Bedroom in the Building

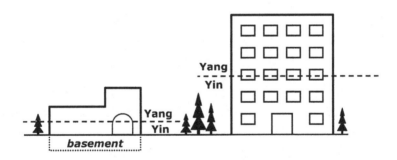

The vertical yin-yang of a building

Fig. 2.4

Basement

If the bedroom is in a basement partially below ground level, it has the advantage of being in a yin location, because it is low in the building. The main disadvantage of this location is that it can have a vibration of "pressure" because the bulk of the space is above it. This is especially a concern in a building that is six or more floors high, and without windows in the basement. This is usually not a serious problem and can be fairly easily fixed by using light.

The best type of light fixture for a basement or other low room is an *uplight*, one that aims the light up, such as a torchiere or wall sconce. Light is energy and when it strikes the ceiling it symbolically pushes it up and away, thus relieving pressure. The simplest uplight is a can light, a type of directional spotlight that is in effect "a light bulb in a can." They are inexpensive and available at hardware and lighting supply stores.

I generally recommend clear light bulbs for any type of uplight as long as the bulb is not seen by the eye. The force of the light is a bit more yang and powerful than with frosted bulbs. Also, if it looks appropriate (or is completely unseen), use some kind of pointy bulb, such as a flame tip. That way, even the shape of the bulb is symbolically pushing away the pressure from above.

A clear light bulb makes distinct shadows. You can take advantage of this by using floor lights to illuminate plants from below. This projects shadows of natural forms and beauty onto a surface that is fairly plain in most homes. By putting light and shadow onto the ceiling, you are activating the yang part of the room. Subtle lighting is yin, which is restful, and is very appropriate in the bedroom.

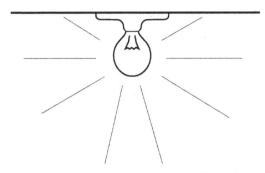

Standard light bulb on ceiling

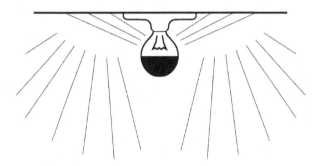

Silver tipped bulb on ceiling
Fig. 2.5

If the main light of the room is one light bulb in the center of the ceiling you can convert it into an uplight by using a silver-tipped bulb. Then, the light that reaches you will have been reflected from the ceiling, as in Fig. 2.5. Silver-tipped bulbs may not be appropriate in every instance, but if they are, they sure change the *feel* of the room. If it makes the room seem dimmer, it may not be the right kind of bulb for your situation. It depends on what other kinds of light are in the room. It is usually best to paint ceilings white or a very light pastel color because light is reflected better. A dark ceiling often feels oppressive, as if chi is bearing down.

Radon gas is radioactive and can cause lung cancer. The gas is produced by the decay of radioactive radium in the earth's crust, and it's one of the most dangerous toxic substances. Radon is not a problem in most homes, but basement rooms should always be tested. If you suspect gas, do a test. You have two choices of test kits available at hardware stores: charcoal canister (cheaper and less accurate) or the alpha track detector (accurate, but costly). If I slept in a basement, I'd use an alpha track detector, especially if there were exposed brick walls. (Bricks have an above-average level of radon gas.) Experts disagree about whether or not sealing cracks has any effect, but all agree that ventilation is key. Airtight buildings trap radon gas inside, so more radon is available to be inhaled. Average buildings used to have a complete air turnover five times per hour—now it's only once every five hours in "tight" buildings. Fresh air is good for you.

Ground Floor

Bedrooms on the ground (first) floor are extremely common, and fortunately they don't pose any feng shui problems unless there are more than (about) six floors above them. If there are many floors above them, uplights are called for. Use them as you would in a basement situation as described in the previous section.

Bedrooms on the ground floor (as well as basement bedrooms) can benefit from having a fairly light-colored floor or rug. This is also the case in rooms with many floors above them. The lightness of the rug lifts the energy of the room. In a one-or two-story house, however, that is probably not a concern.

Up to Four Floors

Bedrooms on the first four floors of a building do not have any inherent feng shui problems based on their location in the height of the building. It's nice to be able to say that, because that's where the vast number of people sleep.

A problem in some modern homes is the proximity of electric wires. If you can look out your bedroom window and see electric wires within thirty feet, you may have strong electromagnetic radiation. See Chapter 7 for more information on EMFs.

You may have heard that some Chinese people dislike living on the fourth floor or at any address with the number four in it. In Cantonese, the word for "four" and the word for "death" sound similar. If Cantonese is not your first language, this connection has no validity. The number four is excellent in any part of an address, just as is any other number. The system of numbers helps us find locations via addresses. End of story as far as I'm concerned. I don't practice numerology. Suit yourself on that.

Fifth Floor and Higher

Bedrooms that are quite high in a building benefit from having at least one (and preferably several) very heavy objects in the room. A very heavy object (such as a large stone sculpture or a marble table) acts as a solid grounding force—the bigger the better, without being too extreme. Heavy objects work best if they are placed low in the room, preferably on the floor.

A high bedroom should have some heavy and substantial-looking furniture. Dark furniture (such as walnut) is preferred to light (such as bird's-eye maple). The bed, especially, should seem well connected to the floor.

If there's a carpet or rug, it should be somewhat dark. A white or very light rug is too airy, and has "float-away" energy. The darker floor color is more grounding.

High-rise bedrooms are a fairly recent invention in the history of humanity. There is another fairly recent invention that helps counter the negative effects of sleeping so high up—a magnetic mattress pad. It usually fits under the regular mattress, and provides an even, negative magnetic field for the body. More information on these mattress pads is in Chapter 4 under Materials. Although magnetic mattress pads are especially useful in high-rise bedrooms, you do not have to live in a high bedroom to enjoy their extra restful effect. There are several fine manufacturers. See Sources.

Chapter 3

Location of the Bed

For some people the title of this chapter will elicit the comment, "As if I have a choice!" In some bedrooms there is no choice—only one wall looks and feels right for the bed. Anything else would simply not work.

It is important that where you sleep feels right. Intuition plays a vital role in the placement of the bed, but there are also feng shui rules that should be observed. It is helpful to know the reasoning behind the rules.

Empowered Positions

As chi enters a room, it brings with it the aspect of that which is new. When you are aware of the door, you are aware of what is coming into your life. When you are able to see the door (without moving your head more than ninety degrees), you have empowered yourself and strengthened your natural extrasensory perception. If you can't see the doorway, you have disempowered yourself and set yourself up for surprises.

The number-one rule is to be able to see the door easily from the bed. The door represents the future. When lying in bed with your head propped up on a pillow, you should be able to see the main door into the room. If you have to crane your neck to see the door, you are setting up a dynamic in your life that can cause things to surprise you. Events will seem to "come out of left field" and you won't be prepared for them.

An empowered bed position

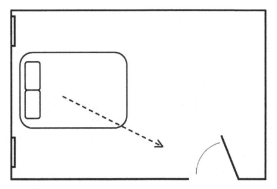

You can easily see toward the doorway.

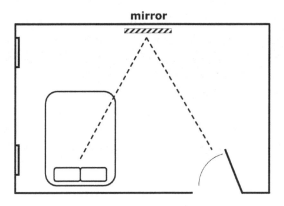

Mirror placement to see the door

Fig. 3.1

Sometimes it is too awkward or impractical to place the bed in the correct position. In this case, use a mirror to see the door. Put the mirror at the right height and angle so that if you are lying in bed, the reflection of the doorway is plainly visible in the mirror. In some instances, that means angling the mirror so that it looks bizarre. A large freestanding dressing mirror is perfect, because it can be easily adjusted and looks natural in the room. You could also use a convex mirror or a large silver gazing ball instead of a flat mirror. But you should not use a convex mirror to check your hair or see how your clothes look. If you use a convex mirror, try to arrange things so that you won't be tempted to use it for that purpose. Seeing oneself clearly in a mirror is akin to knowing oneself clearly. If your reflection is distorted, it will be more difficult for you to have a true awareness of who you really are. Gazing balls are an excellent alternative and fit well in many decors. They are silvered reflective balls intended for use in a garden. Nicely mounted, they look great indoors. They even come in beautiful colors. If you use a colored gazing ball, be sure it is just as reflective as the silver ones.

Be aware that Compass School feng shui is different from the Form School that I practice. In Compass School people are advised to sleep with their heads toward their "lucky direction" based on birth date and numerology. I never recommend that because I don't practice that type of feng shui—and that advice is one of the main reasons I don't practice that kind of feng shui. Some people believe that their heads should be to the north when sleeping to align their body with the axis of the Earth. And some people believe the exact opposite—that feet pointed to the south will devitalize the body. When asked about this, I always say the same thing, "Be able to easily see toward the door of the room."

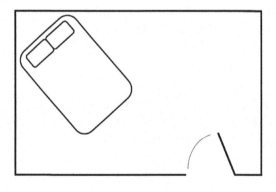

Bed at angle

Fig. 3.2

Some feng shui consultants like to see a bed placed at an angle in the corner of the room as in Fig. 3.2. Other consultants, myself included, prefer that the headboard be placed against a solid wall. When the bed is at an angle a stagnant space is created behind the bed, and there is less symbolic support behind the bed. A solid wall is a very strong thing and having that behind you when you're sleeping is quite powerful. If the bed is at an angle and you want to keep it that way, I recommend having a real growing plant in the space behind the headboard. Because the plant is actually growing, it is not stagnant. A small spotlight shining up on the plant will also help to keep the area from being stagnant. Examples of plants for use in this area are ficus trees and lady palms (*Rhapis excelsa*).

Windows and Skylights

The head of the bed should not be placed directly in front of a window. Locate the bed elsewhere in the room. If that can't be done, just make sure that a heavy window treatment is used each night. Windows that are several feet above the head of the bed are not a problem. The head of the bed can be between two windows, if those windows are on the headboard wall, as in the top example of Fig. 3.1.

Skylights are wonderful, but do not sleep directly under one unless there is some type of pull shade covering it at night. A skylight is a *weak place* in an otherwise solid room. It conveys a feeling of "wide open and out there" and the quality that enhances deep sleep is more "tucked back and sheltered."

Toilet

Do not place the bed so that the head of the bed is on a wall with a toilet on the other side. If there is no other choice, put a mirror behind the bed. The reflective side of the mirror should face the wall. The mirror does not have to be visible.

If a toilet is directly above a bed on the next level up, put a small mirror on the ceiling with the reflective side pointing up. Try to locate the mirror directly under the toilet.

Ceiling

If the bedroom ceiling slopes, the head of the bed should be under the high part of the slope. Placing the head of the bed under the low part of the ceiling adds pressure to your life. The area under the high part of the ceiling is good because there is a natural expansiveness and simply more air.

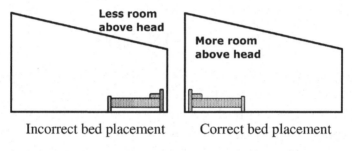

Incorrect bed placement   Correct bed placement

Fig. 3.3

There is a way to symbolically correct or level any sloping ceiling. This becomes especially important if the bed cannot be placed in its ideal location. Hang a faceted prismatic clear crystal from the high part of the ceiling to the level where the wall meets the low part of the ceiling. See Fig. 3.4. I usually use a clear monofilament, like fishing line, to hang the crystal. It is also important to state your intention at the moment of hanging the crystal: "I am hanging this crystal to symbolically level the ceiling" or any other words that seem appropriate. You are not really changing the level of the ceiling. You are doing something symbolic, and therefore your *intention* comes into play very strongly.

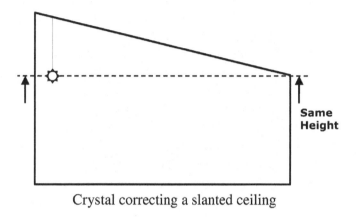

Crystal correcting a slanted ceiling

Fig. 3.4

If you have to put the head of the bed under the lowest part of the ceiling, you can put a mirror and/or a pointy object under that low part of the ceiling, pointing up. They are symbolically lifting the ceiling—the mirror because it reflects up, the pointy object because its energy is physically aimed upward. The mirror can be small like a mirror coaster (or even smaller). The pointy object could be a Sansevieria plant (mother-in-law's-tongue or snake plant), or it could be a stone obelisk or anything similar. See Photo 3.5. An uplight can also be used to symbolically push the low part of the ceiling up.

Upward pointed objects lift energy.

Beams

Exposed overhead beams are considered to "beam down" a pressurized energy. They are responsible for holding up the structure, and there is indeed pressure on them. That pressure influences the energy in the room as long as the beam is seen. All structures have beams, but in most cases the ceiling covers them. As long as they are covered, they are not influencing the room.

The exposed beam causes a problem only if it crosses directly over the bed or a favored lounge chair in the bedroom. If there is no option but to locate a bed under an exposed beam, it is necessary to make the beam go away—at least symbolically.

You can do so by removing the beam if it is not structural, or you can hide the beam so that its shape is not apparent. Use fabric. In some situations it works to have strands of tiny clear lights behind the fabric. The effect is similar to seeing stars through a mist. If lights are used, turn them off when you're sleeping. You can make the beam visually disappear by painting it the same color as the ceiling. If painting is not an option, hang a crystal or wind chime from the beam over the bed or chair.

Sometimes a beam lends itself to having a plant (real or artificial) trail along it or twine around it. It is especially important that the lower part of the beam be covered.

Uplighting, such as a wall sconce or torchiere, can counter the effect of the beam if placed directly under it.

If none of these solutions is acceptable, put a small mirror somewhere discreet under the beam, shining up at the beam. A mirrored tabletop placed directly under the beam reflects the beam and lessens its detrimental effect. Say out loud something like, "This is to reflect away the energy of the beam."

Bamboo flutes are a specific solution for dealing with problem beams. In the majority of my own practice, bamboo flutes, red string or ribbon, and nine inches are not used. Some people however prefer them. Use red string or ribbon cut to nine inches or a multiple thereof, and hang the flutes at a forty-five degree angle with mouthpieces down and toward the walls. The red symbolizes blood, and represents a new beginning, or new blood foundation. Red is a very powerful color in feng shui, and can influence change. The number nine is the highest single-digit number. This conveys strength and can symbolize the strength of the intention. The intention in this case is to lift the energy of the beams. The uplifting sound that a flute can produce helps raise the energy and relieve pressure. Also, air goes into the lower end of the flute and exits through the top end. This signifies uplifting—air pushing up. If it appeals to you, this red-ribbon (or red thread or string) technique can also be used for hanging items such as wind chimes or crystals anywhere.

Door

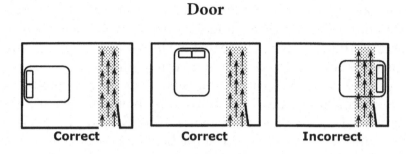

| Correct | Correct | Incorrect |

Bed placement relative to the chi from the doorway

Fig. 3.6

Generally, chi energy enters a bedroom (or any room) most powerfully through the entrance door. There is a swath of strong chi energy about three feet wide (the width of the door) going directly across the bedroom—from front wall to back wall. Make sure the bed is not located in this swath of energy. This particular energy packs a punch, and hopefully there is a way to locate the bed out of its path. It is particularly important not to lie fully in the swath of chi energy with your feet facing the door. That is known as the "coffin position" because coffins are carried through doorways feet first.

If there is no choice but to have a bed located in that swath of energy, some sort of buffer or screen should be placed between the door and the bed. Examples are:

- An armoire or large chest
- A folding screen
- Tall, thickly foliaged plants (even good artificial ones will do)
- A curtain—preferably thick like velvet, but even sheers will work
- A beaded curtain, if that works with the decor
- A thick, patterned rug
- If none of the above or anything similar is appropriate, just hang a crystal.

The crystal symbolizes the intention to disperse the overly strong chi energy before it reaches the bed. Just as the facets of a crystal can cause light to reflect in many directions, they symbolically disperse energy. Be sure the crystal is hanging between the door and the bed, above head height. Hang the crystal with red thread or ribbon if it looks appropriate; otherwise, use clear monofilament. This symbolic kind of feng shui solution is made stronger by expressing the intention out loud. Say whatever seems appropriate. "This is to disperse any harsh energy from the doorway," or "I wish to sleep more soundly." Use whatever words feel right to you. Intention expressed is intention strengthened.

The thread or string should be cut to nine inches, or a multiple of nine, but it does not matter how low from the ceiling the crystal hangs. Hang it a bit low, but not in the way, as crystals chip easily. Lead crystal is softer than glass, so be careful handling it. A chipped crystal will still make rainbows, but it will forever be a chipped crystal and therefore not ideal for feng shui purposes.

Chapter 4

The Bed as a Physical Object

Headboard

A good solid headboard can do two things. It helps bind a relationship, and it represents backing. Even if a bed is not used as a relationship bed (two people sleeping together), it is still important to have a solid headboard (not bars or slats). A solid headboard can instill more confidence in your life by reinforcing the feeling that your decisions are backed up. If the bed is a relationship bed, the solid headboard does more than provide backing. It symbolizes a solid unity. You should be able to look at the headboard and say, "That's how I feel about our relationship, honey—solid!"

This open headboard offers no protection from the protruding angles in the corner. Solid headboards are always best.

Bars or slats (or any headboard with holes in it) represent an open relationship. They are not considered to be conducive to monogamy. If having a solid headboard isn't possible, then sew (or have someone sew for you) a fabric slipcover that will slide down over the existing headboard, and make it look like an upholstered headboard. Examples are in *New Upholstery* in Recommended Reading. The best upholstered headboards have a solid sheet of wood in the very back, like the bed on the cover of this book. If you can't do anything else with an open headboard, intertwine the bars or slats with ribbon, fabric, or strands of silk plants.

Headboards are generally made of wood, metal, or fabric. They sometimes incorporate materials such as leather or mirrors. Since a solid headboard is ideal in feng shui, I recommend wood. Wood is sturdy and solid and brings those qualities into the life of the sleeper. Wood has a friendlier feel; it is not as hard and cold as metal. Solid metal headboards are probably available, although most metal headboards are composed of bars. Padded fabric headboards are a good option, because there is usually some solid wood on the back side, and the fabric has a restful, yin quality.

There are diverse opinions concerning mirrors in headboards. If you don't already have a mirrored headboard, I don't recommend getting one. If you already have one, and don't feel that you are getting your best sleep, try covering it at night and see if you notice a difference. Cover it for at least a month to know for sure. If you have a mirrored headboard and sleep quite soundly, then I doubt it is having an adverse effect.

Be wary of headboards that have a high overhead shelf built into them. Preferably, put nothing on that shelf (over your head) except perhaps plant vines twining together. The plant pots should not be in the area over your head, but off to the side. No heavy objects, such as books, should be on the high shelf. Also be wary of a headboard with an extremely angular design, such as the one in Fig. 4.2. It is too fiery and active.

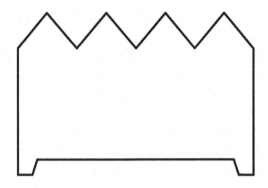

Angular headboard (not recommended)

Fig. 4.2

If you don't want a headboard or cannot get one, consider a headboard substitute. A quilt or other heavy fabric hung from the wall at the head of the bed is a reasonable substitute. It won't be quite as good as a real headboard that is attached to the bed, but if a dark fabric is used, it will sure seem solid.

There are rare occasions when the headboard is larger than the bed and it's not feasible to get a larger size mattress because the room isn't big enough. If you don't want to exchange the headboard for a smaller one you can get metal extension plates that are made just for the purpose of attaching a smaller bed to a larger headboard. The headboard should always be attached to the bed, not just propped up behind it.

Also on rare occasions, I've seen headboards with dragons carved into them. They're gorgeous, but only appropriate in guestrooms, because the dragon is very yang, and its image should not be in the bedroom—especially not near your head.

Footboard

A footboard represents grounding. If there is no footboard on your bed, your feet will symbolically hang out in space for a third of your life. This can add spaceyness to the personality.

The footboard should be approximately the same height as the top of the mattress. If it is too high, as in some sleigh beds, it has a confining quality. The footboard should match the headboard in design and materials.

Of course, a lot of beds are designed to have a headboard only—no matching footboard. If a footboard is not an option, try placing a cedar chest, a bench, or even a dark-colored blanket at the end of your bed. A dark rug on the floor at the foot of the bed is another simple solution.

Mattress

Whatever mattress size is comfortable and appropriate is okay with feng shui. However, the box springs of a standard king-sized bed (also known as an Eastern king) usually consist of a pair of twin-width box springs, which can be a problem. This is inappropriate for a relationship bed because it represents a separateness. The box springs are closer to the floor than the mattress, and therefore symbolize foundation. Such a situation can tend to reinforce the fundamental differences between the two partners. The symbolic solution is to get a red king-sized sheet, and place it between the box springs and the mattress. Try to find a brilliant red sheet, because it will represent a new "blood" foundation. If the king-sized mattress is on a platform, and there are no box springs, there is no problem. Note that the California king-size mattress is longer (by four inches) than the standard king, but it's also four inches narrower and therefore has one unified box springs, so the Cal king doesn't need the red sheet cure.

Be cautious when using an old mattress in a new relationship. Many people let go of the old mattress on a relationship bed when new partners are sleeping there (or when anticipating a new relationship). For some people, it can be important to part with the entire bed. Letting go of old things in our lives opens up the way for new things—and people—to flow in.

If keeping the old mattress is the only option, then clean and air it well. Also, do what's called a clearing. It is usually done for a whole room, but it can be done effectively for any object. Waft white sage incense all around the mattress quite heavily. Speak boldly and assertively saying something like, "Any old vibes must get out now," or whatever words feel appropriate. It is cleansing on a vibrational level and is quite effective for restoring the original purity of a thing or a space. More information on Space Clearing is on page Chapter 16.

I'm a light sleeper and for me the mattress is *everything*. The best sleep I've ever gotten was while using a thick wool mattress pad on top of egg crate foam (with the smooth side up) on top of my regular (somewhat firm) mattress.

No adult who sleeps in the bed should have to stand on tiptoes to sit on the bed. Some high sleigh beds require the use of small matching stairs and it would be better to get a lower bed. Otherwise the symbol is "rest is out-of-reach." If the bed seems too low, you can get bed leg extenders, which are specially made to raise a bed.

Materials

A box springs and a mattress of some kind on top of it are what most folks sleep on. This type of setup usually is some distance from the floor, and that's good. Low beds are not a feng shui favorite. There is a vastly improved model of the ordinary bed called Dux. The mattress is a very thin pad, and most of the comfort and support is from the unique box springs. They are not cheap.

Foam mattresses are not a problem unless they have come brand-new from the factory. When foam is new it can release gaseous chemicals into the air. Once the foam is a few weeks old, the problem usually ceases. If you smell a chemical odor coming from a new foam, that's the cause. Just expose it to excellent fresh-air ventilation for the first few weeks. Don't sleep on a new mattress that has a strong chemical smell. When using a foam mattress, be sure that the underside is well ventilated by turning it over regularly. Memory foam is perfect for some people, but it makes other people sweat and feel too warm.

Cotton futons are natural and very comfortable for some people. They are, however, too firm for others, especially those who tend to sleep on their side. A cotton futon must have good ventilation beneath it or be flipped over regularly. If you live in a damp environment, watch for mildew.

There are two other types of mattress pads that are usually placed on top of your regular mattress. A feather bed is like a very thick feather comforter. It needs to be shaken and fluffed *every day*. A wool mattress pad is **ideal** if you are not allergic to wool. It is soft, yet firm, and allows good air circulation. It is not sheepskin, just a pad of very thick wool.

Some people love waterbeds, and some people never will. If sleeping on a waterbed feels restful and intuitively right, then do it. But make sure if partners sleep on a waterbed that both feel benefited. A waterbed is a large amount of water in a big bag. There are five archetypal "Elements" in feng shui, and Water is one of them. The chart in Chapter 9, shows which kinds of things represent each element. The area around a waterbed benefits from having things that represent the Wood or Earth elements. In this way the Water element is reduced, and the area is more balanced. If a waterbed does not have the ability to lower its temperature at night, you are probably not getting your deepest sleep. Cooler body temperatures are associated with deep sleep. That's one of the reasons not to exercise right before bed—it raises your temperature. There is also a concern about waterbed heaters exposing your body to high electromagnetic fields. You can unplug the heater and put a thick pad between the waterbed and the bottom sheet. The heater can be left on during the time that you aren't on the bed. Unplugging the heater is safer than just turning it off.

An air mattress is rarely a good permanent mattress. The sleeper's body causes the bag of air to be pressurized, and that pressurized vibe continues throughout the night. Use an air mattress only when it is necessary, as when camping.

Magnetic mattress pads are a fairly recent invention, based on the concept of magnet therapy. Magnets are embedded at regular intervals in a pad. The pad then goes under a standard mattress, but not under the box springs. I don't know about the spectrum of magnetic therapy products, but I do know when I rest well. I appreciate the quality of rest I get when sleeping above a magnetic sleep pad. They are expensive, but good sleep is priceless. I especially recommend them for insomniacs. They are not for use by pregnant women, infants, or anyone with an implanted device, such as a pacemaker, defibrillator, or insulin pump. More information is in Chapter 2.

Unusual beds

Platform Beds

Platform beds can be nicely grounding, but they shouldn't extend several inches beyond the foot and sides of the bed. Platform beds that extend beyond the mattress may look sleek and modern, but looks aren't everything in a bedroom, and you shouldn't have to be extra cautious not to bump yourself on your own bed.

Chest Beds

A chest bed has built-in drawers to maximize storage areas. However, the ideal feng shui bed should store only items that relate to the bed, such as pillows and neatly folded sheets and blankets. If other things must be stored under the bed, those things should be emotionally "quiet." No old tax records, no old diaries. Clothes and bedding are less of a problem, because they get laundered regularly, washing away old vibes. It's better to store soft things under a bed, rather than hard things like tools. If hard things must be stored there, put a very small mirror under the mattress facing down toward the storage area. The mirror can also be under the mattress support, accessed through the drawers.

Foldaway Beds

Foldaway beds are a marvelous design solution for multipurpose bedrooms. Because they are put away in the daytime, they retain restful yin vibrations. Ideally a foldaway bed is one that is completely out of the living space in the daytime. A foldaway bed is definitely preferable to a bed that is in the way all day, and gets used as a couch. A mattress that folds into a couch is not bad, but has a bit more yang vibration than a bed that disappears. A futon couch/bed should definitely be folded into a couch in the daytime. There are some sleek modern lounge chairs that can easily be pushed into a flat shape for sleeping. They could be perfect for a single bed in a studio apartment, because they don't really look like a bed at all when they are in the lounge position—but they sure look modern.

Bunks and Trundles

Bunks beds are not ideal. Unless the sleeper is a child, a bunk bed situation is usually temporary—as when you're staying in a cabin. In a dormitory-type situation there is a feeling of impermanence, of wanting a room of one's own. This is not conducive to sound sleep. If bunks must be used, the structural support beneath the upper mattress (the metal links or wood slats) should not be visible to the person in the lower bunk. Perhaps use fabric with a star pattern to cover it. Children sleeping in a bunk bed should be able to sit up in bed without bumping their heads. If that happens, they've outgrown the bunk bed, and it's time to look for different sleeping arrangements. To energetically open the space above a bottom bunk, hang a tiny bell under the upper bunk. Some feng shui teachers recommend that bunk bed occupants trade top and bottom bunks occasionally.

Trundle beds have no inherent energetic problem. The lower bed gets tucked away in the daytime and retains restful, yin vibrations. The upper bed may or may not have some yang energy, depending on how much it is used as a couch in the daytime. Be sure the trundle moves in and out easily without being forced. When children use trundle beds, sibling rivalry can be an issue.

Sleeping Lofts

There are two kinds of sleeping lofts. One is a huge piece of furniture that provides living/work space below the upraised bed. This situation calls for attaching a small mirror to the bottom of the bed, reflecting down onto the most active workspace, i.e., directly above the desktop or computer monitor. If you work in the space below the bed, you should not have an exposed structural beam of the bed above you. Cover the beam with fabric, or see the other solutions in Chapter 3 under Beams. A loft bed (and some upper bunks) can be too close to the ceiling. You should not be so close to the ceiling that you bump your head when sitting upright, or that you cannot move around easily.

An architectural sleeping loft is a semiprivate high room. At least one wall is open to the larger portion of the house, and the area may have a balcony railing. Such openness in a bedroom can be a problem. An obvious factor is whether or not sounds can be heard coming from the rest of the home at bedtime. Make the loft more quiet and private at night if you can. Curtains or Roman shades are possible options.

Many sleeping lofts put the occupant very near a slanted ceiling. The head of the sleeper should be under the high part of the ceiling. In a loft, the high side is usually the side that has the entry. The concern here is that the bed needs to be in an empowered position. The person in the bed must be able to see a person entering, and the bed must not be in a direct line with the entry. Use a mirror if necessary as shown in Fig. 3.1 in Chapter 3.

Both kinds of lofts are commonly entered by climbing a ladder. A ladder usually does not have risers connecting the rungs or steps. An open ladder fails to completely guide chi up to the bed area. Worse things have happened, but it isn't ideal. Steps with risers are great, according to feng shui, but an attempt to visually "fill in" the riser could result in a dangerous and awkward-looking situation, so it is probably best to leave well enough alone.

Floor Sleeping

As you can tell from the last two sections, it's good to have plenty of room over your head when sleeping. That's almost always the case when you sleep on the floor. If a mattress was designed to be placed directly on the floor, that's fine. But if a mattress was intended to be up on a frame, then it should be on one. A standard box spring and mattress should always be off the floor and have a skirt (or something) to connect it visually to the floor. Sleeping close to the floor is recommended by some feng shui consultants as being a grounding thing to do. Some other consultants prefer that mattresses be up off the floor, saying that it's good to raise your sleeping body further away from the low vibe of the floor that is walked on. Tops of mattresses are recommended to be twelve to fourteen inches above the floor, but if you can easily sit on your mattress (and don't have to stand on tiptoes to do so) then it's not too high, and it's not too low.

Canopy or Four-Poster Beds

Canopies can make you feel secure or claustrophobic. Don't sleep in a claustrophobic space if there is any way to avoid it. If a canopy makes you feel secure, then restful sleep will inevitably occur. Some canopy beds have a high structural support that crosses over the sleeper. Try to cover the support with fabric in a way that hides the shape of the support. *If it can't be seen, it's not there* is a handy feng shui trick. If the central support must be seen, it should have a rounded, faceted, crystal hanging from it. A small disco-ball shaped clear lead-glass crystal is best.

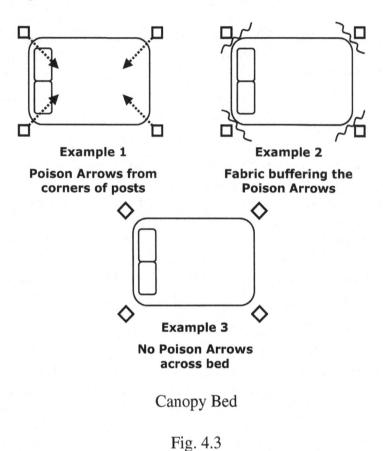

Example 1

Poison Arrows from corners of posts

Example 2

Fabric buffering the Poison Arrows

Example 3

No Poison Arrows across bed

Canopy Bed

Fig. 4.3

Beds with four high square posts, one at each corner, cause an energetic problem known as poison arrows (see Chapter 6). Example 1 in Fig. 4.3 shows the problem. I've only seen one exception—the square posts that usually cause poison arrows were placed so that there was no angle aimed across the bed. It's a very modern look, but very feng shui-friendly—see Example 3. Most four-posters have square posts, or the lowest part of the post is square and the upper part is rounded. Posts that are completely rounded, top to bottom, are best. Otherwise watch out for those square posts. If the post is square to the height of a few inches higher than the mattress, you've got poison arrows—four of them. Pillows or bed hangings can be used to buffer your body from the sharp right angles, as in Example 2.

If the angles on the bedpost are larger than a right angle, there is no poison arrow.

Hammocks

A hammock can provide a restful nap, but is not ideal as a permanent bed. A hammock can cause back problems if you sleep in it night after night. There are two types of hammocks: those with a wooden stretcher at the head and/or foot of the webbing, and those with no stretcher. A hammock with a wooden stretcher is secure only as long as you remain in the very middle of the hammock. It is easy to fall out of this type of hammock. Those without a wooden stretcher are safer because they usually do not have a tendency to turn over and cause the occupant to fall out.

Bed Clothes

Bedspread

Fabric is yin, because it is soft and flexible, rather than stiff and hard, which is yang. But some fabrics are more yin (velvet and chenille, which are fuzzy) and some fabrics are more yang (a slick, shiny satin or metallic cloth). A soft, textured bedspread is a good feng shui choice. The color can be determined by which area of the bedroom's bagua the bed is in. See Chapter 9, The Bagua. If the bed is a relationship bed, try to use warm colors (such as a dusty rose or soft yellow) to symbolize a warm relationship.

It is a good idea to love your bedspread, or at least be very fond of it. Often it is the dominant fabric in the room. If you love your bedspread, making your bed each morning won't seem like such a chore. The bed should be made shortly after rising. Then the old "sleep energy" won't be affecting you when alertness is needed during the day.

It is best not to be able to see under a bed—use a bed skirt or something similar. The bed is more grounded if the floor under it is hidden from view.

Sheets

Soft cotton sheets are ideal in my opinion, perhaps flannel in cold weather. The soft coziness of flannel makes it a perfect yin sheet. If the bedspread is doing its job, the sheets are not seen when the bed is made. Therefore, the sheets could be a color that enhances the area of the bedroom according to the bagua map (as referenced under "Bedspread" above). If that idea appeals to you, go for it. If it is a relationship bed, both partners must be content with the color selection. Because they are so yin, black sheets are extra restful. They represent quiet night. Solid color sheets are visually quieter than most printed sheets and are generally a better choice.

The highest quality sheets are of linen from the flax plant. Two sets of linen sheets could last you for more than twenty years. But the main thing is: "How does it feel to *your* skin?"

Pillows

Pillows must be comfortable and be healthy for your neck. There are many different kinds of pillows and the manufacturers of all of them claim great benefits from the use of their pillows. Use your own judgment. How do you sleep, and how does your neck feel in the morning?

The feng shui concern is more about how *many* pillows are on the bed. Too many pillows amount to clutter. An overabundance of decorative bed pillows is a decorating fad. Try not to have purely decorative pillows on the bed. It is better to like the look of the pillows that are actually used. It's fine to have a bedspread cover all the pillows if there are only one or two. The pillows are then tucked away and remain more yin. Another decorating fad is to give pillows a karate chop, so they have a lived-in look. A dent should be in a pillow because a person's head was there; otherwise keep it fluffed and ready.

Bed pillows (of any kind) should not have hard items sewn onto them, and this includes glass beads. No big hard buttons or other hard objects (with some exceptions for special circumstances) should be on the surface of a bed pillow. Pillows with hard objects are okay for couches, but not beds. Soft things should be emphasized in "the nest." Beware of bed pillows with obtrusive zippers. If you're talented enough to make your own bed pillow (with zippers), use the most curved zippers available, not the ones with the squarer corners.

Blankets

Natural material is preferred for all bed clothing, including blankets. Electric blankets are not recommended, even if they are not plugged in. Electric blankets can influence a sleeper's body whether they are turned on or not. The range of effects is:

- High. The blanket is plugged in and turned on. Even that small electric current is disruptive to the body's own natural electric workings.
- Medium. The blanket is plugged in, but not turned on. This is still not great, because there is still a direct connection between the blanket and the electric system of the building.
- Low. The blanket is unplugged but still on the bed—because the connection to the wall is broken by unplugging, this is quite livable. Many people turn on an electric blanket before getting into bed to make it more warm and cozy, then turn it off. It is best to unplug the blanket, not just turn it off. It is also ideal to remove the electric blanket before going to bed. It would be better not to have the metal wiring so close to your body for a third of your life. To avoid all of this, just use a hot water bottle.

Some electric blankets have no EMFs, even when they are turned on. That surprised me. Pregnant women can sleep under an electric blanket *only* when it is unplugged. Otherwise, the risk of miscarriage is increased.

Bed Hangings

A nest-like bed is a very yin thing—perfect for sleeping. Nothing else gives as much bang-for-the-buck as bed hangings. You need not have a four-poster bed to have a curtain or canopy around your bed. Bed hangings do not have to look like curtains or drapes, they can look simpler, like a screen. If you need some creative input to imagine hangings around your bed, see *The Bed* in Recommended Reading. It shows some modern, but mostly traditional, luxurious bed hangings in wide variety of settings. If you have mosquito netting around your bed, be sure to use one that is made of all natural fiber (usually cotton). The synthetic kind can drop millions of tiny plastic flakes on the bed. I've seen it happen, and those tiny flakes can go into your lungs as you breathe.

If the bedroom has a very high ceiling, the bed hangings should not hang directly from the ceiling because that will give the bed and the room an unbalanced look. Instead they should hang from a canopy bed, and that will make the sleeping space feel cozy and right.

Chapter 5

What Happens in a Bed

People do more than just sleep in a bed. What takes place on or near a bed leaves a karmic residue that can affect the quality of sleep there.

Sleep

The primary purpose of a bed is sleep—any other purpose is secondary. The ideal situation is a bed that is used for sleep and nothing else. Not everyone has that luxury, but if the bed can be used only for sleeping, then do so.

Come sleep time, a bedroom needs to seem like one giant sleeping pill, a space that supports nature's blessed rest. Whatever else happened on or around the bed should feel long gone.

You get your most restful sleep when these three factors are fulfilled:

- Total darkness. If window light can be totally blocked, then do so. Some people will always want a nightlight, and if so, use the lowest wattage available (three watts or less). Dollhouse lights are extremely low wattage and are appropriate in some situations—especially where the light is on a small protective or spiritual image. If there is any light at night, it is interfering with the body's natural release of melatonin. The pineal gland secretes melatonin in total darkness, and the melatonin boosts the immune system and slows the growth of cancers.

- Total quiet. Noise at night is a big problem in certain places. My condolences to you if your bedroom is disturbed by noise. It can make the world seem to be a more hateful place. Noise triggers a blast of adrenaline in the body, and is stressful. Make your bedroom quieter by using a lot of heavy fabrics. Otherwise use earplugs or pillows to muffle noise. Use a masking device (such as a fountain or "ocean sound" machine) only when necessary, because it adds to the noise level, albeit in a minor way. Your deepest sleep occurs on the quietest nights.
- Light air circulation. The ideal is a very light, fresh breeze wafting over you. If noise is not a factor, try to leave a bedroom window at least slightly open at night. Hardware stores sell safety devices to secure a slightly open window. Don't use a fan unless you must, because of the extra sound. However, if you need a fan to remove stagnant chi in hot summer months, place it as high as possible and try to hang a crystal from the base of the fan to disperse the cutting energy of the blades. The new tower fans can have high electromagnetic fields, so don't have them closer than about three feet from the bed.

It is important to know that our deepest, most restful sleep occurs before midnight. If you go to bed earlier, you will awake more rested. Depressed people will probably feel less depressed. Also, do not eat a big meal (a light snack may help some people sleep) or do heavy exercise just before going to bed. Six to eight hours of sleep is generally the proper amount for adequate rest. Sleeping beyond eight hours on a regular basis will likely have an enervating effect on the body.

Dreams are an aspect of sleep. They can be important learning tools in our lives. I recommend keeping a pad and pen by the bed (or an audio recorder) to record dreams immediately upon awakening while the details are fresh in your memory. When writing down a dream, try to keep your body in the same position you were in when dreaming. The book (and audio) that I recommend the most is *The Dream Book* and *Dreams* (audio), both by Betty Bethards. See Recommended Reading.

People get their most solid sleep when sleeping alone, even when they *think* they sleep more soundly with their partner. That's according to the 1994 Longborough study from England. One of the reasons is that your aura is being "recharged", and it can do that best when you're sleeping at least four feet (some experts say four arm-lengths) from another person—that's just how Nature is. Dreams are often more profound and meaningful when you sleep alone. Otherwise you may be taking in some of the other person's conditioning. This includes pets. Sleeping alone (at least occasionally) need not be a sign of relationship discord.

Sex

Whatever happens sexually in your bed is only your business and your partner's business. Some lovemaking is gentle and quiet (yin) and some is boisterous and exuberant (yang). If your lovemaking is boisterous, consider making love someplace other than the place you sleep. There will be a yang vibration lingering on what should be a rather yin bed (for most restful sleep). People who think of themselves as light sleepers can be disturbed by such vibrations more than those who easily fall asleep and stay asleep throughout the night.

If people don't live with you (or with you and your partner), you can move any very boisterous lovemaking from your bedroom into a different room. Do so only if it feels right. The bedroom will then be more conducive to deep sleep.

If you are trying to get pregnant, don't clean under the bed. Leave that area undisturbed until the baby is born. I know of at least four sets of parents who credit that advice to being the thing that finally worked.

Eating

Do not eat in bed on a regular basis. If you truly have no alternative, then be sure to spare a moment at the beginning and end of each meal to be consciously grateful for the nourishment. The two moments of gratitude formally begin and end the meal. The ending gratitude allows the bed to resume its prime purpose—rest.

Couch Substitute

If your bed must serve as a couch substitute, as in many small studio apartments, that's too bad. However, it is often not a very serious concern in the scope of the whole bedroom. If you sleep quite soundly, it is probably not a big deal. If you don't sleep well, try to find a way to put the bed away—even if that means getting a bed that will fold into a couch.

Do not begrudge the extra moments it takes to fold the bed away. Done mindfully, these moments add centering to the day. When the bed is set down for sleep, mindfulness is an introduction to dreamtime. Earlier I suggested not having an excess of decorative pillows on the bed. Only when the bed functions as a couch substitute is it all right to go ahead and use lots of pillows, if that's your style. Pillows (or any decorative fabrics such as a tapestry or afghan) act as a symbolic buffer between the mattress that is slept on and the couch that has a more active use.

Chapter 6

Other Furniture

Bedroom furniture with curves is usually preferred to hard-edged furniture. The furniture with more rounded edges is more yin, and we want to keep thinking *yin* with bedrooms. Try to avoid furniture with sharp right angle corners.

Wood surfaces are better in bedrooms because wood is a softer material than metal, glass, or hard plastic. The bedroom is not the room for glass tabletops because they are very hard and shiny. Glass is a form of metal, and it is best kept to a minimum in bedrooms. Especially don't have glass-top tables where the glass extends beyond the base of the table. The bare glass edge of the table represents a razor to cut you from achieving your goals. If the glass is inset in wood and no bare edge is seen, it is okay. Stone tabletops are also very hard, but if they are surrounded by wood (as with a stone insert) the problem is mitigated.

This glass tabletop does not have cutting energy because the edge of the glass is surrounded by wood.

Poison Arrows

One of the main concerns with bedroom furniture is whether it is causing a poison arrow, and whether that poison arrow crosses over the sleeper's body.

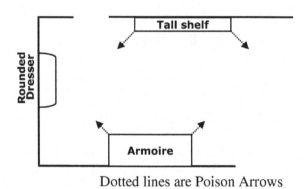

Dotted lines are Poison Arrows

Fig. 6.2

A poison arrow is a line of chi energy that has picked up a negative charge by encountering a sharp right angle. Poison arrows are most often caused by furniture with sharp angles along the vertical edges. To see the exact path of this kind of poison arrow, divide the sharp angle in half and follow where it points. See Fig. 6.2. It is quite specific and if it points out into a space that is only walked by, or rarely sat in, there is no problem. But don't have this type of poison arrow (coming from a sharp right angle) pointing directly at the entry to a room. It is subliminally saying no to people who enter, and it is also saying no to chi energy. Don't spend significant time with a poison arrow aimed at you.

A poison arrow can be stopped by draping the offending edge with fabric. It can also be stopped by placing a substantial object (such as a large plant) between the sharp edge and the bed. If the vertical edge of the furniture is well rounded, or is an angle larger than ninety degrees, as with a six-sided table, there is no poison arrow.

You spend (more or less) a third of your life in bed. A third of your life should not be spent in the path of a poison arrow. The stress of being constantly in the path of a poison arrow can manifest as a health problem. The area of the body that is in the poison arrow's line becomes more vulnerable.

Side Tables

Bedside tables can make serious poison arrows point across the bed. If the side table aims a sharp right angle across the bed as in Fig. 6.3, consider getting side tables with rounded corners. If the side tables with sharp right angles must stay, cover them with a tablecloth. If a tablecloth won't work, put a piece of fabric (towel, shirt, or whatever) over the offending corner when you go to bed for the night—every night. If there are extra pillows on the bed, stuff them between the poison arrow and the bed.

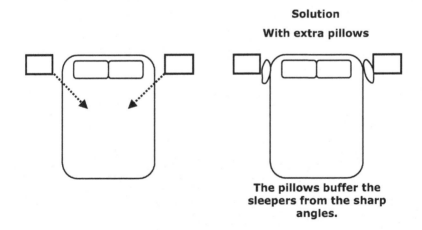

Solution

With extra pillows

The pillows buffer the sleepers from the sharp angles.

Poison Arrows from bedside tables

Fig. 6.3

One of my clients (a widow in her late seventies) surprised me by interrupting my explanation of how to cover up her sharp, right-angle side table. She said that as soon as the consultation was over, she was going to get her saw and blunt that sharp corner. My jaw dropped and I shook her hand. (It was not an expensive table.) Another client said she always woke up with neck pain until she covered the sharp right angles of her bedside tables with washcloths. After that, the morning neck pain was gone.

Side tables should be about the same height as the bed—not drastically lower or higher. Matching side tables are ideal for a relationship bed.

Dressers

Dressers can potentially have two kinds of problems. They can cause poison arrows if their vertical edges are sharp, and they can have mirrors that are a bit on the low side. It is important that the mirror show all of your head when you're seeing your reflection. If the mirror cuts off the top of your head when you are walking around the room or standing right in front of it, it needs to be raised. In a couple's bedroom, the mirror should not cut off either person's head.

Chests of Drawers

A chest of drawers must not point a poison arrow at the bed. It must not seem foreboding by being overly large and dark for the room. If it has a mirror, the same rule applies as with dressers—the head must be fully seen.

Armoires

Everything in the above section applies to armoires. If there is adequate closet space, don't even have an armoire, unless it is used to store a television. Even more than a chest of drawers, an armoire can have a foreboding presence, if it is large and the room is small. If the room is small, it is imperative that the armoire be of light-colored wood and have graciously curved edges.

Chairs

If there is a chair in the bedroom that is frequently used, place it so that the occupant can see the door to the room. Any chairs in the bedroom should seem inviting—soft, warm, chairs are preferred to bare wood or cold leather. If it works in the decor, have the color of the chair be the correct bagua color for where it is in the room. See The Bagua, Chapter 9. If the main bedroom chair is a desk chair, it is good if the back of the chair fully covers the occupant's back. It represents solid backing in life.

It's good to have at least one chair in any bedroom that is large enough to comfortably hold it. That way a person can sit in the room without having to sit directly on the bed. A bed that is sat on a lot is not as energetically quiet as a bed that is rarely sat on. If there is more than one chair in the bedroom, be sure that the room does not look cramped. I've seen otherwise stunning master bedroom suites in which you had to wiggle your way past furniture to go through the room! In most cases, one chair per bedroom is plenty.

Bookcases

Do not have a bookcase in a bedroom unless necessary. Books have a noisy yang vibration because of all their words. If they need to be in the bedroom, they must not dominate the decor. Downplay them. Ideally, put them in a bookcase with doors. In some situations it works to cover a bookcase with fabric.

There is a second reason for covering a bedroom bookcase. If the bookcase is directly facing the bed, the edge of the shelf is sending a cutting energy across the sleeper's body. It is a form of poison arrow, but can be quite nullified by putting a real, from-the-earth crystal (such as quartz) on any shelves that are approximately at the same height as the mattress top. Crystals often have sharp points and those should be pointed away from the sleeper's body. I usually direct the crystal points upward. If the shelf boards are extraordinarily thick (one and a half inches or thicker) there is much less danger of a poison arrow coming from them. A thick wooden lip on the edge of a shelf can serve to "blunt" the sharp energy from the shelf. See Fig 6.4.

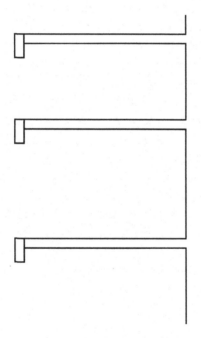

Side view of shelving with lip added
To stop Poison Arrow

Fig. 6.4

If the vertical edge of the bookcase has a sharp right angle, it can aim a poison arrow across the bed in the same way that a chest-of-drawers or other tall furniture can. Preferably, use a bookcase with rounded vertical corners. (There are lots of them out there.) Otherwise, if a poison arrow goes across the bed, be sure that the bookcase corner gets covered every night.

Desks

A small decorative desk that is seldom used is not a problem in a bedroom as long as there is plenty of room for it. An active desk that is used for hours each day is a different matter. Such a desk retains its active yang vibrations. If the desk must be in the bedroom, try to screen it from the bed. Some desks screen themselves by having a roll top or fold top. That type of desk is ideal if the surface is closed away when work is through. If nothing else will work, just drape a nice fabric over the desk busyness before you sleep.

Computer monitors should be covered at night. Any cloth will do, even a T-shirt. But why not make it a nice cloth that you really like. And while you're at it, use a cloth that is the correct color for the area of the bagua in the bedroom. Closing a laptop computer in a bedroom is good enough for restful sleep, but putting it in a drawer or covering it with a nice cloth is even better. Other electronic items that are at desk height or higher should be covered when not in use to keep the bedroom more peaceful. It also prolongs the life of the electronic item by keeping dust out.

Chapter 7

Other Things to Consider in the Bedroom

For a bedroom to feel peaceful, it doesn't necessarily need to have a lot of things. But it does need some things—all rooms do. The first things that make a bedroom feel right are a door that will close and a window that will open.

Windows

Bedrooms need good ventilation and some sunlight—but not too much sunlight because that will make the room be too yang. Just as circulating air removes stagnant energy, so does sunlight—and sunlight brings happiness. If sunlight never enters the bedroom, be sure to leave the window open often to refresh the room.

The ideal window in feng shui is one that opens fully and completely, as opposed to one that can only open partway at a time. Windows, like doors, allow chi to enter your life. Windows that open fully allow you to reach your potential more easily. The vitality of fresh air is chi energy. Let it into your bedroom. Do not have windows that rattle or are painted shut. Windows should be fully functional—otherwise there can be a dysfunctional tendency that isn't easily overcome. Also, keep your windows clean. Clean them at least twice a year. Windows represent your inner eyes, your ability to know what you should be doing in your life. Clean windows allow you to do that more fully.

Hopefully the view is pleasant outside your bedroom window(s). If it isn't, consider installing a window box. They are easy to install and transform a view quickly.

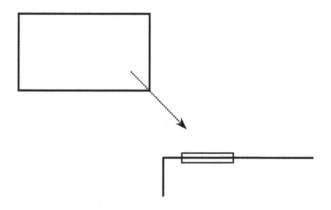

Poison arrow from neighboring building
into bedroom window.

Fig. 7.1

From your bedroom window, you should not see the right-angle corner of a building (or other large object) pointed directly toward you. Fig. 7.1 is an example of that situation. If there is any sharp or foreboding building or object pointing at the bedroom window, put a mirror outside to exactly reflect the building (or object). A small flat mirror will do or you could use a convex mirror, because then you don't have to aim it exactly. The bulge of the convex mirror reflects more of the view. The "poison arrow" that a sharp right angle directs toward your bedroom can also be counteracted by hanging a clear faceted crystal in the window. (I recommend octagonal crystals for windows that get sunlight—they are the most prismatic.) When using a mirror you would say something like, "This is to reflect away the influence of the angle of that building." When using a crystal you would say something like, "This is to disperse the influence of that building before it affects the bedroom."

If there is a very busy road outside the bedroom window, definitely use a convex mirror to reflect away more of the road traffic. If the mirror cannot be put outside the window, put it inside the window facing out. It should still be reflecting the foreboding object, and be as close to the windowpane as possible. It is fine to use a very small mirror. Car headlights should not be able to shine into a bedroom at night—use a blackout shade if necessary. Those lights are considered to be "invading" your space.

If a church, mortuary, or cemetery is directly next door and visible from the window, put a mirror outside to reflect it—a bagua mirror is best in this instance. (In these three instances, also make sure to keep a light on a sacred image at night.)

Do not have bare bedroom windows! Use some kind of window treatment to shut out neighborhood light. Brightly lit neighborhoods have been linked to higher rates of breast cancer in women. If there is no neighborhood light, use curtains just to cover the black hole of the window glass at night. Drapes and curtains are preferred to Venetian or vertical blinds because the fabric is softer, and drapes and curtains cannot aim a blade of cutting energy into the room.

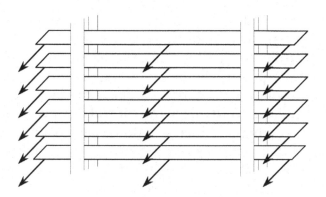

Poison arrows from Venetian blinds

Fig. 7.2

Blinds can easily slice up the air in the room with lots of cutting energy. Each louver is a symbolic blade. Trace the path of that blade into the room to see where the slice is aiming. See Fig. 7.2. Adjust the louvers so that they do not aim their blades at you when you are spending time in your bedroom. It is not important how the louvers are aimed during the time that the bedroom is not much used (i.e., during the day for most people).

If you need privacy out your bedroom windows, but still want to see blue sky and nature, use shades (or blinds) that are mounted on the bottom sill and pull up to obscure just the part of the view that you *want* to obscure. These kinds of shades are also perfect for bedrooms with floor-to-ceiling windows, because energy tends to leave those rooms too quickly. The shades act as a sort of wainscoting, and should be used as such most of the time. Café curtains are a less expensive alternative to pull-up shades.

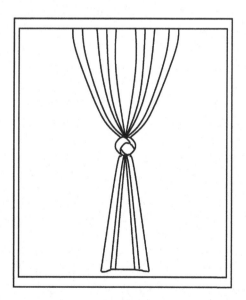

Not this way

Fig. 7.3

If a window has a single panel of curtain covering it, be sure not to tie the fabric in the middle of the window and leave it hanging like that, as in Fig 7.3. A single curtain panel that has been tied in an obvious knot (in the middle of the window) can say, "Things are in knots—not going smoothly." The curtain almost looks as if it's committing suicide. Use some type of tieback and pull it to the side instead of into the middle of the window. It usually looks more natural to pull the single panel toward the side of the window that is closest to a corner. If the window is in the middle of a wall, draw the panel toward the more "restful" part of the bedroom—toward a bed. When a curtain has been knotted for a while, it's going to need ironing. Curtains that are pulled to the side don't usually have wrinkles when they are unfurled. An unwrinkled curtain has a more peaceful feeling.

Heavy window treatment does not appeal to everyone, but I believe it would appeal to more people if it didn't seem so costly in time or money. Good, heavy window treatment is the job of a professional or someone (you?) willing to learn. Heavy means thick material, lining, and even interlined drapes (where a third fabric is sown in between the lining that faces the window and the nice fabric that you see). Interlined drapes are the ultimate yin drapery, but even if you can sew, you might not want to attempt them unless you have experience in drapery making. You also need a huge workspace, because everything needs to stay straight and flat.

Here are four more items that can be added to bedroom window treatment, if they appeal to you. They won't appeal to everyone, but if done well, they can give a bedroom a very nest-like feeling.

- Valance—this is very important in horizontal windows
- Tassels—there are incredibly beautiful tassels, all kinds
- Fringe—especially very thick, long fringe
- An excess of fabric

The fabric excess can be done with lots of folds—even in the valance, if it looks good. It can also be done through pooling the drapes on the floor. The pooling is good feng shui because it symbolically gathers the lower chi and directs it *strongly* upward.

Don't rule out heavy window treatment for the bedroom unless you have exposed yourself to some good examples of its use. There is an abundance of fine books on window treatments. One such book is *Winning Windows* (see Recommended Reading).

If heavy window treatment doesn't appeal to you, perhaps something modern like heavy Roman shades would work. If it is difficult to obtain the desired degree of darkness in the bedroom, consider installing a blackout roller shade behind the more decorative window treatment.

When a bedroom window is directly opposite the door to the room, the chi that enters the bedroom is likely to vanish quickly out the window. Sheer curtains will keep the chi in and allow it to circulate within the room. A small decorative mirror is also a good idea. Place it on the wall above the window, facing into the room. It symbolically reflects the chi back into the room. Also a decorative object such as a crystal, wind chime, or mobile can be hung from the ceiling between the door and the window.

When a bedroom window is only partially opposite the door to the room, a different problem is created, know as a "split view." Easy solutions to this problem are in the first section of Chapter 10, The Shape of the Bedroom.

A regular-sized window at the foot of the bed isn't a problem, but if a very large window is at the foot of the bed some consultants recommend the use of heavy window coverings at night so that chi energy is conserved while you rest.

Doors

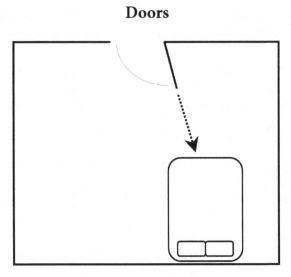

Poison Arrow from door

Fig. 7.4

A door, even a cabinet door, can aim a poison arrow into the room. To see how this kind of poison arrow can happen, see Fig. 7.4. Wherever a door points to in room is where the poison arrow is pointing. The solution is to open or close doors fully. It is best for the bedroom and closet doors to be closed while you are sleeping. But leave the bedroom door open for safety or ventilation if you need to.

Doors in general represent opportunities, and the bedroom door is an especially important door/opportunity. If the hinges squeak or if the door sticks against the floor and won't open fully, the symbol is that opportunities will be more difficult to find. It's easy enough to oil hinges, but if the door sticks, you may have to take the door off the hinges and sand down the bottom of the door.

The bedroom door should be able to open all the way to the wall, with of course a doorstop to keep the knob from dinging the wall. Double doors are never recommended for bedrooms, no matter how large. They allow too much energy to come into a quiet room. If you only use one of the doors, it's as if you are giving the other door an inferiority complex, so use both doors occasionally. If you can afford it, have the double doors replaced with one nice single door.

Occasionally a bedroom door opens into a corner so that the first thing you see as it opens is the adjacent wall. That's not the best way to hang a door. The door hinges should be on the other side of the doorframe, so when you enter the room the first thing that's noticed is the *openness* of the room. If the door cannot be rehung, put a mirror on the wall so that as the door opens the reflection of the *openness* of the room is seen.

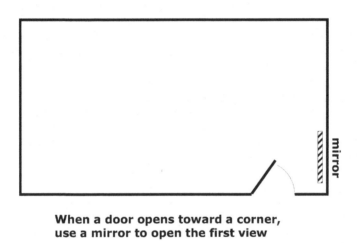

When a door opens toward a corner, use a mirror to open the first view

Door opening into corner

Fig. 7.5

If a bedroom has more than one door coming and going into the rest of the house, the bedroom runs the risk of developing a "hallway" vibe—or, where you could keep walking in a circle, a "racetrack" vibe. That's too yang and active to benefit the purpose of the quiet bedroom. Try to keep at least one of those doors closed most of the time. It's also a good idea to hang a disco-ball shaped crystal in the bedroom, in the pathway between the two doors, to symbolically disperse the busy energy. See Fig. 7.6.

This is especially important if the two doors into the bedroom are across from each other on opposite walls in the bedroom. Especially, don't have a bed placed between the two opposite doors. A very small wind chime can be used instead of a crystal. When you hang the crystal or chime, say out loud that you are symbolically dispersing energy.

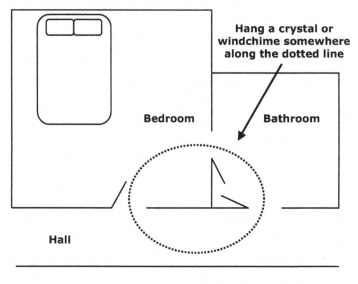

Bedroom as hallway

Fig. 7.6

If the knob of one door can touch the knob of any other door, you have a situation known as "clashing knobs." The knobs symbolize heads butting against each other and add a vibration of conflict or argument. If you live alone you might assume that there is usually no one around to argue with. Well, you can always argue with yourself, and that means having a difficult time making up your mind. Sometimes it is possible to simply hang one of the doors on the opposite side of the doorframe. If that can be done, the situation is fixed completely. If that cannot be done, then learn to love red ribbons. It can be hard to love red ribbons. They sure can look awkward in many homes, but they are a powerful feng shui tool. You can even tie one end of a ribbon to one knob and the other end to the other knob and then cut the ribbon. You have thereby made the knobs related. (Note: the bathroom doors in Fig. 7.6 don't clash, because they can't quite touch.)

Red symbolizes new blood—a fresh beginning. It is commonly used in feng shui whenever a change is needed, but is impossible to do. Tie the red ribbon to any knob that can touch any other knob. At least two knobs get ribbons, and sometimes four knobs depending on how the doors are configured. Items that can be used instead of ribbons are yarn, very thick thread, or tassels. It does not matter how far down the ribbons actually hang once they are tied. At the moment of tying the ribbon, have your intention in mind (to reduce conflict), and say it out loud using whatever words feel appropriate. In my own practice I almost always recommend tassels instead of ribbons in this situation. A red ribbon can look like "Why?" but a fabulous red tassel can look like "Why not!" Try Internet shopping to see a variety of red tassels.

The view out through the bedroom door, when leaving the room, is quite important. What do you see just when you are leaving that room? Most bedroom doors open into a hallway. Ideally, what's directly across from the bedroom door is either a wall or a closet door. It is less than ideal for a bedroom door to directly or partially face another bedroom door. If that's the case, hang a crystal in the hall outside the bedroom door, as in Fig. 7.7. A mirror is also a solution if two doors partially face each other (a split view).

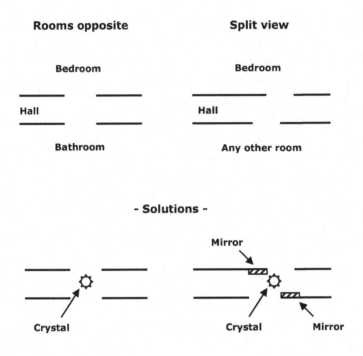

View from bedroom door

Fig. 7.7

When you are walking out of your bedroom doorway, and directly in front of you (before you turn to go down a hallway) is a bathroom door—there should be a *crystal* hung in the hallway between the two doors. Its job is to disperse the energy that might come from the bathroom before it zips right over into the bedroom. Keep the bathroom door closed as much as possible, and put a small mirror above the door in the hallway. The reflective side of the mirror is out toward the hall, to symbolically reflect away energy from going into that bathroom in the first place.

The door to the bedroom should not be at the direct end of a long hallway, as if the hall were aiming energy into the bedroom. If that's the case, hang a crystal or wind chime in the hall, outside the bedroom door. You could also hang a small mirror above the door, reflecting the energy away from coming into the bedroom too harshly.

Wall Color

If it's just *your* bedroom, it can be your favorite color. The exception is blue, which should be used in extreme moderation by those who are prone to depression. You could also paint it the appropriate bagua color for where it is in the whole house. If painting all four walls, use a gentle, easy-to-live-with color.

If one wall will be a bright accent color, it's best if that color is appropriate for the bagua areas that are on that wall. Usually I recommend that the wall behind the headboard be the accent color wall, because the color gives the wall more strength. You are mostly concerned with the *room* bagua, but also keep in mind the bagua of the whole house. It's fine to use a vivid color for an accent wall, just don't use a brash color (such as "fire engine red") in the bedroom—it is too jarring. Gray is an excellent color to pair with a more vivid color, and there are plenty of warm shades of gray.

If you share the bedroom with another adult, you need to find a color that is enjoyed by both of you—and it should be a warm color, symbolizing the warmth in your relationship. So even if it's white, it should be a *warm* off-white—with just the slightest amount of yellow, red, or a warm brown mixed with the white.

Use matte paint finish for the bedroom, because it's more yin. There are even paints that dry to be a little fuzzy, like velvet—perfect for a yin room. It's good if the wall surface is sound absorbing—it makes the room more yin. Wallpaper, with a subtle pattern, or even wall cloth are good options in bedrooms. Wall cloth can catch dust, and require more attention in cleaning that a simple painted wall. But, if well done, it is the perfect wall surface for a restful bedroom—a heavy linen perhaps. Other than unfinished wood, wall cloth is one of the few truly natural wall surfaces. Don't use metallic wallpaper in a bedroom because it's too yang. It's fine to use a flocked wallpaper in the bedroom, because the fuzziness is nicely yin. Wallpaper or cloth feels very natural above wainscoting. (Wainscoting should generally be darker than the color above it on the wall.)

Fabric is fine for the ceiling too; either draped high over the bed or for the entire ceiling. Ceiling colors should be a white or a lighter shade of the wall colors. The only time it's appropriate to use a darkish ceiling color is when the ceiling is so high that it feels out-of-proportion for the room.

Support Poles

Central support poles symbolize a split view—"Here's my way of seeing things and there's your way of seeing things" (on the other side of the pole). Central poles can also make furniture placement very difficult. Always try to make a pole visually disappear by placing something tall next to it. Make sure the tall object is secure from falling. This is a real solution, because you've really made the pole less noticeable. If it's not feasible to put a tall object next to the pole, put at least one mirror (shiny side out facing the room) on the side of the pole. You are symbolically erasing the pole and that's what you need to say out loud when you do this cure.

Most bedrooms don't have freestanding support poles (vertical structural support columns), but some do. I recently was at the home of a single woman (with a disagreeable neighbor) who had an awkward support pole in the middle of the bedroom. The couple that lived in the home before her had gotten divorced and it had been their bedroom. She had her bed placed against the pole so the bed was in the middle of the room, far from ideal, but she had good reasons for wanting to keep it that way. I suggested that she put a shoji screen at the head of her bed to lessen the visual effect of the pole. The screen would also act as a symbolic headboard, because the bed had no headboard.

Mirrors

Mirrors are very multipurpose in feng shui. They expand a space and bring in fresh energy. They repel menacing objects and poison arrows, and they keep chi from quickly vanishing out a window. Mirrors also symbolically seal off one area from another, such as a bathroom from a bedroom. Mirrors can "bring back" a missing area, if the floor plan of the room is not a perfect square or rectangle. See Chapter 10, The Shape of the Bedroom. Another use of mirrors is to empower you when you have your back to the door.

Mirrors are quite controversial in bedrooms, especially mirrors that reflect the bed. Some feng shui teachers warn against them, citing such things as disturbed sleep and unfaithful relationships. Others praise mirrors in bedrooms, saying they lessen tensions and improve relationships. My biggest concern with mirrors in bedrooms is how well the person sleeps. If there is a history of disturbed sleep, I recommend that you remove mirrors from the bedroom, or cover them before you sleep. Try it as an experiment for a few months to see if sleep improves. If you have mirrors in the bedroom and sleep soundly, I doubt that the mirrors are causing any problem. Instead they could be bringing an expansiveness to your life.

Do not have a mirror in a Fortunate Blessings area (back left corner as seen from the bedroom door)—see Chapter 9, The Bagua. A mirror represents a window. This is especially true when the mirror reflects the view from a window, as when the window is on a wall opposite or at a right angle to the mirror. However, mirrors located anywhere in the room (even a mirrored tabletop) can represent a window. Windows of any kind are a "leak opportunity" for chi. That leak is mainly a problem when it occurs in a Fortunate Blessings area. The fewer windows in a Fortunate Blessings area, the better. The fewer mirrors in a Fortunate Blessings area, the better also.

A mirror is always okay in a bedroom is when it is used to reflect the door, so that someone in bed can see the door. It is preferable not to arrange the furniture so as to create that kind of situation in the first place. But sometimes there is no other option. More information on using mirrors to see a doorway is in Chapter 3, Empowered Positions.

Mirrors indicate how truly and honestly you see yourself. They should always be clean and in good repair—no cracks, no bad silvering. A cracked mirror gives you a fractured image of yourself, as do mirror tiles or any mirror that breaks up the image. Old mirrors with bad silvering cannot give you a true reflection of yourself, and may contribute to low self-esteem. If the mirror is an antique, the bad silvering actually adds to the value of the piece, and if that's the reason you own it, here's my suggestion: have the old glass removed, save it, and replace it with new mirror glass. If and when you sell the piece, put the bad mirror back in. The value is preserved, but you haven't had to live with the consequences of bad silvering for all those years. New mirror glass is not expensive. Avoid mirrors of smoked or colored glass. Some mirrors have designs etched or painted on them. It is best not to view yourself in such mirrors on a regular basis. If the design is just around the border, the mirror is probably okay.

If a mirror in the bedroom is used to see yourself, it should show all of your head. If all of the head cannot be seen, you may experience problems such as headaches or unclear thinking. Ideally a mirror should also show the space eight inches above your head, because that represents your potential. A bedroom mirror's ideal shape is round or oval. Those shapes are more yin, whereas square or rectangular shapes are more yang. The only mirror shape that really shouldn't be in the bedroom is a triangular mirror, which is much too yang, and they are fairly uncommon anyway.

Televisions

If possible, do not have a television in the bedroom. It doesn't belong in there if there is any other acceptable place to put it. This is one thing that all feng shui teachers agree on. Too much screen viewing is common in homes, and the bedroom should have a more restful vibration.

If a television must be in the bedroom, then cover it when it's not in use, or have it in a cabinet that can be closed. If you use the television to help you get sleepy and turn it off with the remote control, this can lead to disturbed and garbled dreams. There are other ways to promote sleep: read, meditate, reflect on the day, or chat with someone close to you. Use your imagination. An expensive solution to a television in a bedroom is to have one that vanishes out of sight at the push of a button. Here's the bottom line: If you get sound sleep with the screen uncovered, then it is probably not having an effect on you. Covering a television (or computer monitor) when it's not in use is a bold statement about priorities in your life. The priority of the bedroom must always be good, solid rest.

Unless the television vanishes out of sight, something should be hung on the wall above it—hopefully, something you like a lot. It's meant to distract the eye away from the television when it's not turned on. (It's almost impossible to distract the eye from the television once it's on.)

If a wall-mounted television is in a bedroom, it should definitely be the flat-screen kind. The older kind of television has a foreboding quality when mounted overhead on a wall, especially if someone has to walk or sit under it.

Electromagnetic Fields (EMFs)

If an electrical panel (fuse box or breaker box) is on a wall directly outside a bedroom, the bedroom should be checked with a gaussmeter for high EMFs. Gaussmeters are available on Amazon for as low as $15. Sometimes the EMFs from the fuse box disappear after a few feet or inches, but sometimes the entire bedroom has an electromagnetic field that is much too high for a person to safely spend significant time in.

No one should sleep with a cell phone under their pillow. Even when it's turned off the cell phone regularly has an elevated electromagnetic field as it stays in contact with the transmitting tower.

The safest computer screen (especially for children) is a flat panel, as on laptops. Children grow at a faster rate than do adults. Therefore their cells are dividing more frequently, and are more susceptible to factors that can cause the DNA not to reproduce correctly. DNA problems can be extremely serious. I have measured the electromagnetic radiation that comes from both kinds of computer monitors, and the old-fashioned kind (with the cathode ray gun that protrudes in the back) has severely high EMFs for about three or four feet. The flat screens don't usually have measurable EMFs, because the technology is so different. The main EMF problem with laptops is that there is a strong EMF reading above and below the keyboard (where the working guts are). When a laptop is turned on it should never be sitting on a person's lap, otherwise your lower organs are being zapped. The high EMF only extends about four to six inches, so prop it up if you're going to have the laptop in your actual lap. Use a breakfast-in-bed table or an overly thick pillow with a board on top, so that the laptop can still ventilate from below. Your fingers are almost always getting a high amount of EMFs and run the risk of developing bone cancer there, so it's best to use a separate keyboard that either plugs into the laptop or is wireless.

E-book readers, such as Kindle, don't have measurable EMFs at all (in my experience), neither do Bluetooths, iPads, or iPods. It seems that the electronics industry is slowly becoming aware that consumers are educating themselves about the dangers of high electromagnetic fields. I believe, in the future, we will see personal electronic devices with practically no EMFs.

Occasionally a client has an electric massage chair in their bedroom, and when I see it I say, "Oh, you have an electric chair." I ask them to turn it on and I put a gaussmeter where their body would be and *always* the needle tries to go off the dial. The EMFs of electric massage chairs are very dangerously high, and they are right at a persons' vital organs. Some of these chairs are fine as long as they are turned off, but some have high EMFs unless they are actually *unplugged*.

Some consultants prefer that aquariums not be in the bedroom. If the person sleeps well with an aquarium in the bedroom, I don't see it as a problem, as long as it's not close to the bed or a chair where the person spends a lot of time. An electric aquarium pump has very high EMFs, but they only extend a foot or two away from the pump.

Small devices are sold which purportedly undo the effects of high EMFs. None of these devices reduces the measurement of EMFs on a gaussmeter, so in my opinion they all are (expensive) bad science. The only thing that can shield you from a nearby high EMF is a sheet of solid metal. Food wrapping foil is not thick enough, but sometimes a cookie-baking sheet is thick enough.

Clocks

Bedroom clocks should be silent when running—no loud ticking. They should show the time accurately (within a few minutes). A clock that does not show the correct time brings the vibration of untrustworthiness into your life. If a clock is stuck and doesn't work, have it repaired or get rid of it. If it's a sentimental clock you could also put it in a box, label it, and store it. Clocks that are stuck in the past are holding you back in the past.

Bedside clocks are best placed on bedside tables. If there is a shelf at the head of the bed, do not place a clock in the center part of that shelf. Also, do not place a wall clock at the foot of the bed.

Digital clocks that plug into a wall socket (such as clock radios) often have a surprisingly powerful electromagnetic field (EMF). The field can be measured to determine how far the clock should be from a sleeper's body. Gaussmeters for measuring EMFs are available (see Sources). The meters aren't cheap. Perhaps a cardiologist would lend one to you. To be on the safe side, make sure any plug-in digital clock is several feet from the your body. Most importantly, do not have the clock close to your head.

Books

It is fine to have a few books in the bedroom, just not too many. The bedroom should not resemble a library. Do not have a lot of books or magazines near the bed, such as on a bedside table. Two or three books is plenty there. Books contain words and thoughts, and are considered busy. If many books must be kept in the bedroom, try to keep them out of sight—see Bookcases in the previous chapter.

If hardback books are kept in view, consider removing the dust covers. The dust covers help sell and protect the book when it is in a store. Once you own the book, the dust cover can be removed, and there you'll often see a lovely cloth binding (nicely yin) with attractive lettering. The actual binding of a hardback is not only more elegant than the dust cover, it is visually quieter. This is how the book is supposed to look in your home. It says that you own it. Do not discard the dust cover. It usually contains information about the author that is nowhere else in the book, and the dust cover is 90 percent of the book's resale value. If you're storing a lot of dust covers, I recommend filing them in a box in alphabetical order by book title. However, if the books are in a sunny location, keep the dust cover on them. Otherwise the book covers will fade.

Dolls and Collectibles

Dolls and plush animals are not appropriate in view in adult bedrooms on a regular basis. This may seem harsh to some and logical to others. See Children's Rooms, Chapter 12.

Any collection of "collectibles" would be better in a more yang room, such as a family room or living room. Collection refers to a large number of similar small decorative items that serve no purpose. Almost any collection possesses a busyness because of the quantity of the items, which are often quite detailed. Collectibles (except weapons) are fine in bedrooms—just not a whole collection of them.

Lamps

Bedroom lamps can be simple or fancy, but avoid using lamps that have sharp right angles, because they can create poison arrows. Lamps, like nightstands, must not aim a poison arrow at a sleeper's body, so if the lampshade is square, turn the angle so that it does not aim toward the bed. See the illustrations in Chapter 6, Other Furniture. Round or rounded lampshades are preferred in a bedroom. Avoid lampshades with *actual pressed plants* (or leaves) in the paper, because they can symbolize "dead and dried-up."

Fabric or paper shades are softer than metal or plastic. Generally, they would be better for bedrooms. A relationship bed should preferably have matching lamps on each side. Bedroom lamp color should be muted, rather than vivid. The color of the lamp can be related to the *bagua area of the room* that the lamp is in. See Chapter 9, the Bagua. Also, Chapter 8 concerns lighting in its many forms, not just lamps.

Exercise Equipment

Exercise equipment has a yang quality because its use is active. Even exercise equipment that is seldom used has this quality. Ideally, exercise equipment should not be kept in the bedroom, but we don't live in an ideal world, and sometimes there is no other option. Exercise equipment that is kept in the bedroom should be stored out of sight. A screen is perfect, but small bedrooms may not have enough room for a screen. It is okay just to drape nice fabric over the equipment. It's best not to store exercise equipment under the bed, especially if you are a light sleeper.

Plants

A moderate number of plants can be an energetic asset in the bedroom. They can be artificial or real. Artificial plants do not add the etheric vibrancy (and oxygen) of real ones, but do use them if they appeal to you and look appropriate in the room. Artificial plants must be dusted—and washed—every so often to stay looking good. Run them under a shower. Cheap-looking plastic flowers are not preferred; better to use quality "silk" flowers.

Don't use dried plants as decoration in the bedroom unless they get changed at least twice a year and preferably once every season. Dried plants are dead, and their energy reads dead. Live chi energy once flowed through them as sap. The sap is gone and they begin to rob you of your vitality and hold you back in the past. Some people like to keep dried flowers from sentimental occasions. It is truly not a good idea. Let them go back to the earth. Fresh energy with your name on it has been waiting for that moment. Artificial plants do not have this stagnating quality since sap never flowed through them. Potpourri is commonly used in bedrooms but is not recommended because the flowers are dead and are often scented with synthetic perfumes. A freshly made potpourri with natural oils is fine, and can be used for many months.

Spiky houseplants are almost never recommended in feng shui. Avoid any plant that you wouldn't feel comfortable going up to and shaking hands with. This is especially true in the bedroom. Grow plants with rounded leaves in the bedroom. If there is a windowbox outside a bedroom window, its plants should also emphasize rounded leaves.

Plants that are particularly appropriate in bedrooms are those with fuzzy leaves, such as:

- African Violets, which bloom almost constantly.
- Purple Velvet Plant *(Gynura aurantiaca)*. It is easy to grow, but can get leggy if not pinched back.
- Teddy-bear Plant *(Cyanotis kewensis)*. This plant likes to trail down, but don't have an overabundance of drooping plants. They can bring a feeling of depression.
- *Kalanchoe.* There are several Kalanchoes with wonderfully fuzzy leaves: *tomentosa, beharensis,* and *belutina.*

Another delightful plant for a bedroom with a bright window is the Polka-dot Plant *(Hypoestes phyllostachya)*. Even when it isn't blooming, it looks very attractive, with pink splashes on green leaves. It is a perfect plant for the Relationship area of a bedroom, the far right corner—see The Bagua, Chapter 9.

Animals

One or two pets are okay in a bedroom, but preferably not on the same bed as the people. Pets have small, but very *powerful* auras. People get their truest dreams by sleeping alone. I have to say that's a hard message to hear, and I don't enjoy saying it, but I do believe it. If an animal sleeps in the bedroom, make sure the room gets an abundance of fresh air. It will be good for everyone, people and pets.

Fountains

Fountains involve water. Water is yin when it is compared to dryness (which is yang). But there is very yang water (Niagara Falls) and very yin water (Okefenokee Swamp). A fountain is yang because it is active—probably too active for most bedrooms. Do not put a fountain near the head of the bed even if it is turned off at night. Fountains are always fine in guest rooms. In a guestroom that activity is welcome, since the room can have a stagnant energy because it is used infrequently. When guests are staying in the room, show them how to turn the fountain off at night. If possible, place the fountain in the Fortunate Blessings corner of the bedroom.

Fountains are often appropriate in a studio apartment, but they should be turned off when someone is sleeping. See Chapter 13, Studio Apartments.

Fountains are also good for masking noise. I'd take a good fountain over a "noise machine" any time.

Plants, cats, and birds love fountains. It makes their environment more natural. Cats appreciate drinking the moving water, and birds love them for bathing.

Here are some fountain-shopping tips:

- Fountains that have a light bulb in the water (or very close to the water) represent conflict. This is because the elements Fire and Water are conflicting elements. See Elements, Chapter 9. A spotlight shining on the rippling water is fine because it is not in close physical proximity to the water.
- For the same reason, a fountain with a fogging machine is not recommended. The fog is caused by intense heat.
- Be sure that the pump motor noise is *very* quiet. Silent is ideal. In the quiet of your own home, any motor noise is more noticeable than it is in a store. In the store, put your ear right next to the motor while it is running. If it sounds noisy there, it will sound a lot noisier in your home.
- Make sure the oversplash is well contained in the catching basin. The motor should be turned up fairly high to have lots of splash sound, but if there is oversplash on wood furniture, the furniture surface will be damaged. Make sure there is no oversplash or that it is on a hard surface, such as marble.
- A fountain should not aim a single stream of water into a basin. That's a bathroom sound. A babbling-brook sound is quite different. It is caused by many drops splashing on different levels.
- The very best fountains are those in which the pool of water is still visible when the motor is turned off. Then the fountain never really looks "dried up." The pool of water represents a pool of resources in your life. In some fountains, all the water vanishes through pebbles when the motor is off. That kind is not preferred.

Allow a fountain to flow all the time if it will not irritate anyone. Fountains work best in feng shui if they run constantly. It does require a commitment to replenish the water regularly because of evaporation.

Altars

It is fine to have an altar or shrine in the bedroom, especially if you want one and there is no other appropriate spot in the home. A bedroom altar should be simple. The simpler the better, generally speaking. If possible, the altar should be at heart level or higher. Try not to place the altar directly opposite the foot of the bed. Such a position has your feet pointing toward the sacred image, and that is considered disrespectful.

Whether or not you have an altar in your bedroom is not really a feng shui concern. However, in the unlikely event that your bedroom window opens out onto a cemetery, you should do something to counter its effect. At night, keep a small light on an image that you feel is sacred or protective. If a nightlight is too bright for your taste, consider using a tiny dollhouse light. It's an appropriate size for a small image.

A sacred image should not look like the place you store your jewelry collection. Also, do not put things in the hands or lap of a Buddha statue—the exception being the picture of a deceased or sick person or animal.

Pictures

If the bedroom is just used for sleeping, do not hang too many pictures. The ideal might be one per wall, with some walls having none. If your decorating sense tells you to put up more pictures, then do so, but not to excess.

Pictures behind glass are okay in bedrooms, but if it is feasible, try to have some of them not behind glass. Glass is hard and slick and thereby quite yang. Non-glare glass is more yin than regular glass. It diffuses reflected light and brings a pleasant softness to the bedroom. Non-glare glass works best if it directly touches the picture. It is also fine to have one layer of matte, but if there are multiple layers of matte the artwork will be less distinct.

To use feng shui principles in selecting the imagery of the bedroom pictures, see The Bagua, Chapter 9. Don't use pictures (or sculpture) with missing body parts (such as the Venus de Milo) unless the artwork is a bust or a head portrait. Something like a bust of Nefertiti is fine because it was intended as a bust (i.e., nothing got broken off). If a picture shows most of a body, but not the head, it probably should not be on display. Also don't display pictures of ruins. They say that your glory years are a thing of the past.

If you don't want to be single don't have pictures of single people of your gender in your bedroom. The same is true for figurines.

The view from the bed is important because it is what you wake up to. It represents the future. You should like the view at the foot of the bed. Sometimes the view is just closet doors. Oh, well, just keep them clean. If the view at the foot of the bed is a blank wall, consider putting a picture there that you truly love. If the bed is a relationship bed, both people should love the picture equally—no compromise. If the view is a split-view (part of the view is of a door going to a bathroom, etc.) put something nice up high that is the full width of the bed. An example is a long lovely cloth that then unifies the view. It doesn't have to cover the door—it can be fully above the door.

It's not uncommon to see wedding pictures in bedrooms. It would be best if they were eventually (within a few years of the wedding) put in a photo album. More than most pictures, wedding pictures are about capturing "a moment in time." You don't need to see that "moment in time" to honor your vows. Be grateful if you have a partner. Be kind and loving every day, and move forward together through life gracefully.

Dragon pictures and images are representing an extremely yang energy—dragon energy. For that reason, they are not recommended in bedrooms.

Abstract art is not a feng shui favorite, simply because some of it is disturbing. Leave disturbing art in galleries and museums. If the abstract art is obviously peaceful, then it's okay. Here's a quote from the classic *Abstract Art* by Michel Seuphor, "The nonformal painters of the present day, for example, turn out works that can serve at most as material for psychiatric case histories." Peaceful representational art is always preferred in feng shui, and for the bedroom, it's best if there are no people or animals that are obviously awake in the picture. Plant pictures and landscapes are generally best in the bedroom.

Rugs and Carpets

Feng shui approves of wall-to-wall carpet in bedrooms if it works in your situation. It absorbs sound, especially with a pad under it. It also adds a yin softness that helps the restful purpose of the room. It is fine to put beautiful rugs, such as sculpted Chinese rugs, over plain carpet. But the rugs must not slip. A rug over a carpet can tend to slide around. In that case use a special plastic pad that grips both, and holds the rug in place. The pad is available at rug stores and some hardware stores. A rug can last *hundreds* of years longer if it has a rug pad under it. A rug over plain carpet is fine, but a rug over other rugs is sometimes not fine. It can be too busy and chaotic if the rugs are of very different styles. If the styles are similar there's probably no problem with rug on rug in the bedroom, as long as nothing slides.

If the bedroom floor is bare at least try to have a bedside rug. Have one on each side of the bed if two people sleep there. If the rugs slip (at all) use nonskid pads under them. Rugs that slip say that you do not have a steady foundation. Round or oval rugs are especially nice for bedrooms because of their yin quality.

If a dragon image is in a rug that rug should be hung, because it's considered disrespectful to step on a dragon image.

Under the Bed

The area under the bed should ideally be empty and unseen. The bed should not appear to be floating in space. With a bed skirt (or a platform bed) the bed becomes more connected to the earth, and more grounded. That groundedness will be conveyed to the sleeper. A bed skirt is also an opportunity to bring more fabric into the bedroom and make it more nestlike. It's common to make the bed skirt fabric and color match the curtains. You'll be tying the room together visually and making the bed more grounded at the same time.

Having the area under the bed empty is not practical for everyone. If things must be stored under the bed, always use appropriate boxes or drawers. They help seal away the objects. Bed leg extenders are available to enlarge the storage space under the bed, but don't use them if they make the mattress too high. You should not have to stand on tiptoes to get your rear end on the bed.

Store soft things such as fabric, not hard things such as tools. Clean bedding can be stored under the bed as long as it is in boxes or drawers. Don't store things that require active or thoughtful use, such as exercise equipment or paper with words on it, including books and diaries. Also, don't store shoes unless they are organized in boxes with lids.

Smell

How a room or dwelling smells is very important. Smell can be considered to be an "object" because what is being inhaled are tiny particles of something. Needless to say, that something should be pleasant in the bedroom (and hopefully in all rooms). If there is a good fresh-air smell already present, I would consider not messing with it. Fresh air is ideal.

If it seems good to add fragrance to a bedroom, aromatherapy has a lot to offer. Aromatherapy is a kindred art to feng shui. It is a recent name for an ancient art, studied by many cultures. Diffusing essential oils is the most often-recommended technique in aromatherapy books, as well as using scented candles or potpourri. Incense is also commonly used by those who don't mind the bit of smoke. Fragrant plants in and around the bedroom are a special delight. These are fragrances which aromatherapy associates with relaxation: lavender (the number one choice by far), rose, patchouli, jasmine, chamomile, narcissus, frangipani (plumeria), cypress, clary sage, and neroli.

If a scented candle doesn't say on the label that the fragrance is natural, then you can be sure it's artificial. If you use artificial scent you're adding petrochemicals to the air of your bedroom, and creating nice-smelling air pollution.

It's best if the bedclothes don't smell like anything. If they smell like detergent, then you are probably breathing a perfumed, chemical off-gassing all night long. Launder sheets and pillowcases in unscented detergents, which are available at natural food stores. Don't use fabric softener on them, and if possible dry them outside in the sunlight.

One smell that is important to avoid in the bedroom is the off-gas from new synthetic objects. Synthetic carpets and carpet pads are usually the worst and the chemicals (volatile organic compounds—VOC) linger in the air much longer than you might suspect. Any new plastic object that has been packaged in tight plastic needs some time to off-gas before you put it in the bedroom, especially close to the bed. Also items made of new plywood or particleboard need time to off-gas. If you can smell it, you are breathing chemicals, and they are never good for you.

Sound

Sound is not precisely an object, but it sure is tangible. Less is better when it comes to restful sleep. The only time that sound is beneficial during sleep is when it masks a more disturbing sound. A fountain is sometimes a suitable remedy for obnoxious traffic and sidewalk noise, but do not add sound to an already quiet bedroom when sleeping.

When no one is asleep in the bedroom, you can use sound. A fountain on a timer is sometimes a happy addition to a bedroom, especially in a studio apartment. Usually fountains should be turned off when someone is sleeping. If televisions can be kept out of the bedroom, they should be. Their sound is considerably more yang than most radio. The sound of a fast-action movie leaves a residual yang energy. The opposite end of the audio spectrum is soft music—very yin—very appropriate for a bedroom.

I hope you do not hear the sound of a refrigerator humming from your bed—this applies mostly to efficiency studio apartments. It's not good to have to hear that (unless it's masking even worse sounds). A refrigerator can be put on cushioning feet to reduce its audio impact in the room

If more than one person sleeps in the bedroom, and one of them snores, it can be quite disturbing. If someone is disturbed by the snoring and doesn't sleep well, something should be done. I'd be a millionaire if I could snap my fingers and make the snoring go away. Alas, it's a sore point in many relationships, and I wish you well to sort it out as compassionate adults. Sleeping in separate rooms need not hurt a relationship. Not getting good sleep can kill a person. Sound affects you although it may not wake you. Even if a person is not awakened by the noise, sound of 35 decibels raises their blood pressure significantly and prevents deep sleep. If someone knows of a safe herbal thing that's good for snoring, please let me know so that I can spread the word.

If neighbor noise is disturbing the peace of your bedroom, put a small mirror against the wall of your bedroom, with the shiny side facing the noise—it is symbolically reflecting the noise away from the room. Tiny mirrors from a craft store are perfect for this. The mirror can also go on the floor or ceiling if that's the direction of the disturbance. If the neighbors are *extremely* disturbing, you can use a bagua mirror instead of a tiny mirror. Make sure the shiny part of the bagua mirror is facing the disturbance, so if it's inside the shiny side is facing the wall. It's best if the bagua mirror can be placed outside. The trigrams on the mirror represent perfect order. Instead of a bagua mirror, you can use a mirror with a six-pointed Seal of Solomon drawn on it. (See Sources for these mirrors.) That symbol also represents perfect order, and has been used in India for millennia to create balanced mandalas.

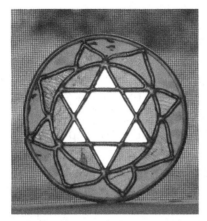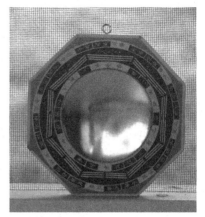

Seal of Solomon mirror on the left and Bagua mirror on the right.

There is yet one more remedy that feng shui has to offer when all else fails and you have the world's most horrible neighbors. You can aim a pointed object at them, but only do this remedy with love in your heart. What you're doing is injecting love into the situation. If you have hatefulness in you heart, you can expect that to boomerang and affect you badly. The pointed object should be large, like a railroad spike, and when you place it say out loud, "I'm injecting love and compassion into the situation" or words to that effect. If you have trouble finding love in your heart but you still want to use this cure, try to imagine how miserable it must be to be the other person. Let empathy develop in your heart and sympathy will follow. I've heard many success stories from people using this technique. Remove the pointed object when the situation has resolved and when it feels right to do so.

Clutter

I believe that the energetic effects of clutter can be devastating to your body and spirit. Being well organized will improve your life in more ways than you can imagine. I am not overstating it to say that having a good sense of structure about your daily life is a great aid to accomplishing the true purpose of your life. If clutter seems to be a major challenge, I recommend Stephanie

Winston's audio *Getting Organized*. See Recommended Reading. Learning is enjoyable and audios are a great way for busy people to continue to learn. You can listen to them while bathing or driving or at other times. Play an audio at least half a dozen times and you really do start to get the message—it sinks in deeply and becomes part of you.

The number one rule of clutter (especially paper clutter) is to stop bringing it home. You undoubtedly control most of the paper clutter that enters your home. Be ruthless. Even if it means canceling the newspaper—don't bring more paper into your home! Some of the most helpful tips are in Jeff Campbell's *Clutter Control*. (See Recommended Reading.)

The number two rule is to make an appointment with yourself (daily if possible) to clear clutter and get more organized. Two habits—television watching and newspaper/ magazine reading—often eat up a person's time and attention and can cause indefinite postponement of clutter clearing.

If you are a television watcher and you have any kind of clutter problem, turn off the television, and leave it off until you are a well-organized, on-top-of-it person. It won't kill you not to watch television so that you can do something more important: clear the clutter. If you are watching a lot of television, please reclaim your life. There is great purpose and potential in every person's life. It is doubtful that watching television is an expression of that purpose. No one should structure their daily life around watching certain programs at certain times. There are many video recording systems that are easy to program and use.

Everyone has a mental "to do" list. It is powerful to write down your list. It is much more powerful to check off the items when they are accomplished. Use the time you've saved by not watching television (or reading magazines) to get organized and accomplish your greatest goals. Use feng shui and get there faster.

Where do you start the process of removing the clutter? Begin directly at the door of the room, and expand out to a three or four foot radius of clutter-free zone. Chi energy should pour freshly into your bedroom through the doorway. Clutter that is very close to the doorway has an immediate stagnating effect on that fresh chi. The subliminal message of the clutter is, "Do this—do that!" The chi energy picks up that message and falls flat on its face. Clear the doorway area so that fresh, enriching chi can flow into your bedroom. It will consequently flow into your life.

The other place to begin is in your Fortunate Blessings corner. Yes, there are two places to begin. Consider both of them to be equally important. Other names for the Fortunate Blessings area are Intention and Empowerment. If it is your intention to live a clutter-free life, the message rings powerfully from this area into the rest of the room. It acts as a psychic gong, ringing in the new clutter-free vibration.

Do not let clutter be reflected in a mirror—it is then symbolically doubled, and made more daunting. If things are cluttering up your life but you can't bring yourself to part with them, remember this rule: the more things you have, the less time you have. It is so true. Unless you are actively using an object or love it dearly, you might want to part with it, even if it was a gift. It is especially unfortunate for a bedroom to look as if items are hoarded there. Sometimes that happens when things get stored in a bedroom during a temporary transition, and that's life. But if things are really being hoarded in the bedroom—if collecting has gotten way out-of-hand—take action! If precious items are in the bedroom, be sure that they are kept properly so the things are not ruined. See *Saving Stuff* in Recommended Reading. Beware of indiscriminate consumption, it's bad for the earth and it can choke up your life. Try to only make purposeful purchases. Think before you buy: "Do I already have a place in mind to put this object?"

Every object in a room has a voice and is making a signal. A bedroom is quieter and more peaceful if there are only a few things in the room. Especially don't have a meaningless display of objects, just because they make the room look "decorated." Have things that you cherish. It's possible for a bedroom to feel too bare, but if there's carpet and very nice, appropriate, window treatment that both go well (color-wise) with the bedspread, you don't really need much more than just the bed. That degree of minimalism isn't good for everyone, but it's a huge statement about the real purpose of the room.

Details

Broken things in your space represent something not working correctly in your life. Anytime you have a broken item in your bedroom, fix it or put a red dot on it. The red symbolizes change, and is a physical "thing" that represents how you wish your space to be—you wish the thing weren't broken. Say your intention out loud when putting the red dot on the broken object. "This [name the item] is symbolically fixed and does not affect my life in a broken way." Use your own words and consciously pick words that you identify with. There is no need to ever repeat your intention; you can now forget about it. Never use this red dot technique on any item where safety is an issue. Common sense tells a person that the item is not physically fixed—miraculously. The red dot is just a symbol—if safety is an issue in a broken item, fix it. How could feng shui recommend otherwise? Your physical space represents the larger aura of your body and life on this planet. It is like a physical prayer—and you're praying for wellness.

If a wall socket has two outlets (and most do), both the outlets need to work. If this isn't feasible (because you're a renter, perhaps) then put a plastic plug cover in the outlet that doesn't work, so that no one would be tempted to use the broken outlet.

Your bedroom does not have to be picture perfect at all times to have good feng shui. A look that is "too perfect" can be nerve-wracking to maintain.

One important final detail is *security*. In many neighborhoods both doors and windows should be locked. All the good feng shui in the world is not going to protect you if you're careless in the wrong neighborhood.

Chapter 8

Lighting

The quality of light greatly influences the energy of the bedroom. Interior design acknowledges five kinds of lighting. (See *Lighting Style* in Recommended Reading.)

Ambient light is the main light (usually overhead). It is the light you would use when cleaning the room. Windows often provide the main ambient light during the day.

Task light is used for specific tasks. A lamp on a bedside table provides light for reading. Lighting around a mirror illuminates your face.

Accent light provides visual interest in a room. A spotlight aimed at artwork accents the piece. A spotlight on the floor behind a plant and aimed up is a fine way to use accent light.

Decorative light refers to a light fixture that is decorative, such as a chandelier or a beautiful stained-glass nightlight.

Kinetic light is light that moves. This refers to anything from a fireplace or a candle to a television or computer screen.

Each type of lighting raises specific feng shui concerns.

Ambient Lighting

The ambient light should be adequate for you to clean the room well. The room should not be so dim at all times that it feels depressive. At least during the day, the room should be able to be bright. However, a bedroom can be too bright, by having too many windows. Windows are a wonderful source of light and fresh air, but direct sunlight pouring into a window is very yang. Many large windows and glass doors hinder the restful yin energy. Every bedroom should have at least one window, but not too many windows. Floor-to-ceiling glass in bedrooms is definitely not recommended! If there are lots of windows, use lots of drapes (or equivalently heavy and soft window treatment—Roman shades, for instance) at night. If a bedroom has lots of sunlit windows that remain uncovered during the day, it may not be truly restful at night. The residue of the bright yang sunlight remains in the room. It might be best to cover some of the windows during the day—if only using sheer curtains.

The ambient light at night is often a combination of several types of lighting. A bedside lamp (task) and a corner uplight (accent) can provide adequate, subdued ambient light for this yin room. If the bedroom is multifunctional, the lighting should be adjusted to the room's current use. When a desk light (task) is turned off, it signals that the desk energy (active, thinking—yang) is not present. When only candles are burning (kinetic—but very yin), it signals that peace and quiet are predominant. Ideally the ambient lighting should be easy to adjust. This is often as easy as installing a dimmer in the light switch of the overhead light. The room can be bright for cleaning or trying on clothes, and it can be dimmer for a quiet time before sleep. Be sure that the dimmer does not cause the light bulb to hum or buzz. Not all dimmers were created equal—most dimmers create a low buzz unless the light is turned up all the way. This is true of even the most expensive dimmers. I have expensive dimmers; I was assured they wouldn't make the light bulbs buzz, and still the light bulbs buzz. In my experience, lighting made by Juno has proved to have absolutely no buzz in our home when a dimmer was installed—specifically TC1 Housing with the 16-WH Wall Wash fitting, a low-profile ceiling spotlight that shines on a wall. It is our favorite room to meditate in, largely because of that one dimmable light fixture—without any buzz at all.

If the bedroom has an overhead light in the center of the room, note the shape of the finial. The finial is the metal tip that screws on and holds the glass light shade in place. The finial should be well rounded. A sharply pointed finial can direct a poison arrow into the center of the room. This is especially troublesome if the bed is directly under the light fixture. There are many styles of blunt or rounded finials available at hardware stores, lighting supply stores, and online. Only the finial needs to be changed, not the whole fixture. Be aware that there are two screw sizes for finials.

If the there is a ceiling fan with several bulbs that aim off toward different areas of the room (each with its separate glass shade), be sure to put rounded bulbs in the sockets. Flame-tip bulbs should not be put in such a fixture, because the points then aim down at people. In nature, flames generally go *up*, like a candle flame. It's best not to sleep directly under a ceiling fan, since the blades represent a cutting energy as well as a hand spread out above you, ready to press down on you. If you have no choice but to have the bed under a ceiling fan, use a crystal to represent that the foreboding energy of the fan blades is dispersed before it reaches your body. Hardware stores sell a type of fan pull that looks like a disco-ball shaped, faceted, crystal. If the fan has a pull chain on it, substitute the crystal ball pull chain. Some ceiling fans have the light fixture part in a frosted bowl, and they don't usually have a pull chain. In that case, take down the bowl, put a small clear, faceted crystal in the bottom of the bowl and then put the bowl back. Be sure to say out loud why you are doing it—to disperse harsh energy before it reaches you. It's also good if the color of the ceiling fan blades matches the ceiling color so that the blades are less noticed. If the blades look like real woven palm leaves, there is no harsh energy coming from them—they are energetically harmless.

It is best if there is no light bulb over the bed at all.

Task Lighting

A bedside lamp is the most obvious bedroom task light. Its task is to provide light for in-bed reading, perhaps the most common pre-sleep activity. When the bedside light is on, it is an energetic pull to come to bed. Other possible task lights in a bedroom might be a lamp by a reading chair, or a desk lamp. A combination of task lights can make a softer ambient light than a stark overhead light. A desk lamp is the one task light that I suggest turning off when the task is finished. As long as the desk lamp is on, it is causing an energetic pull to the desk and its yang busyness.

Accent Lighting

An accent light does not have to shine on an object per se. It can just be a splash of light along a surface of the room. If the room is painted a rich, saturated color, an accent light can let its beauty be more appreciated at night.

A can light behind plants is an easy way to bring accent lighting into the bedroom. The pot of the plant can hide the light, and the ceiling and wall get great plant shadows. If you don't have a green thumb you can use good artificial plants. This can bring fresh chi into what may have previously been a dark, dreary corner. More information on can lights is in Chapter 2, Basements.

Decorative Lighting

Decorative lighting can be a bit on the yang side. It says "notice me." A decorative light is any light that is distinctive and lovely enough to stand on its own as a decorative object. Examples of decorative lighting are: a chandelier, a Tiffany-type stained glass shade, or a seashell light. A chandelier is rarely appropriate in a bedroom. It has an unmistakable "look at me" quality that pulls chi energy up and makes it more yang. Chandeliers made of many cut crystals are never recommended anywhere, because the light is uneven—that kind of wall shadow is not seen as auspicious. An exception would be a simple chandelier of actual candles, which have a romantic yin quality, appropriate for a bedroom. Other decorative lights are unmistakably yin. These include nightlights and any variety of cute small lights illuminating lovely colored glass or plastic. Often the shape is beautiful, such as a turtle with a colored glass shell and a small bulb inside. Such lighting is yin because of its subtlety. It is good to put decorative lights on a quiet timer so that you don't have to think to turn them on. They come on in the evening and they go off at bedtime (as a good reminder).

Here is an example of decorative lighting in an unusual bedroom situation. Jill was having trouble with her teenage daughter. It didn't take a psychic to feel the lousy vibes in the daughter's bedroom. The biggest reason was that the only bedroom window was exactly on the property line, and the neighbor's wall was about four inches on the other side of the glass. The window got no light. It was a window onto "perpetual night." The solution was to hang strands of tiny, clear holiday lights on the outside of the window. Possibly even better would have been tiny lights that had the option to move, such as the kind that slowly blink on and off.

If you like the idea of tiny, clear lights, feel free to use them in various ways in the bedroom. They are unmistakably romantic. If they are kept on a quiet timer, they are easier to enjoy. Changing the settings on the timer to match the seasonal light changes connects us to the natural cycle of the earth's rotation. Also those tiny lights' turning off is a very sweet reminder to go to bed.

Kinetic Light

The ideal kinetic bedroom light is natural—candles or a fireplace. However they are not possible, appropriate, or even desirable in many instances. Candles must be used with the same awareness that you would have of a stove burner that is turned on. Candles could conceivably burn down the house. They probably won't, and they usually don't, but do be careful. Do not burn candles near curtains. Be wary of using wooden candlesticks unless there is a metal insert that fits around the candle base. If you use candles as decoration in your bedroom, be sure you place them where they won't cause trouble. Candles with wood shelves a few inches above them are potentially dangerous. When a candle is not in use, it does not have to be in sight. But if an unlit candle is in sight, it should be where, if it were lit, it would be safe.

Eight-hour votive candles are one of the safest kinds of candles. So you don't break their glass holder, burn the candle fully at one time. If the candle is extinguished then re-lit, the glass heats too quickly and is likely to crack when the wax is almost gone. The votive candle holder can be the correct color for the bagua area in the room. (See the next chapter.) A candle that burns in a glass container can cause black soot from the inside of the glass. This is especially a problem with tall glass prayer candles. Keep that black soot wiped off between burnings. Thick candles burn down in the center, leaving a wall of wax surrounding the flame. Use a nonserrated knife to trim that wall of wax level with the bottom of the black part of the wick. The trimming is best done soon after the candle has been extinguished. The wax is soft, and it is easy to remove the excess wax down to a smooth, level surface. Such a candle will enhance its environment, and when it is relit, will be brighter. Do not display candles with an unburned wick. Unused candles count as clutter. Burning the wick, if only once, says the candles are of use. Ideally, candles should be of a natural material such as beeswax, should not be scented with synthetic perfumes, and should not have a lead core in the wick. If you don't have good air circulation, don't pollute your bedroom air with a chemical fragrance, and notice when extinguishing a candle, if some liquid is needed to make the wick stop smoking. That smoke smell can linger without fresh air to blow it away. If a candle has a lead core wick (and most votive candles do) it will be obvious after the candle has burned for a while. A round black blob will form at the very top of the wick. The concern with lead core wicks is whether or not lead vapor is added to the bedroom air. The composition of the wick is not a big issue if the room has good air circulation.

Fireplaces can provide romantic kinetic light even without a roaring log fire. Gas fireplaces make a gentle, kinetic light that is appreciated any night. If the fireplace is not plumbed for gas, it is usually quite safe to insert a blazing collection of candles. Such kinetic lighting transforms the bedroom.

If real fire is not feasible or appropriate, a very low-watt flicker bulb behind a translucent screen can be kinetic and decorative at the same time. It can gently light up a part of the room that seemed dark and stagnant beforehand.

Any other form of electrically generated kinetic light in the bedroom is most likely coming from a television or computer screen. Neither is preferred in the bedroom according to feng shui. If they must be in the bedroom, do not keep them on unnecessarily or use them as background.

When dealing with kinetic lights, keep the motion slow and gentle. That makes the lighting more yin and more restful for a bedroom.

Light Bulbs

I don't believe that fluorescent bulbs have a place in the bedroom, and this includes compact fluorescents. They flicker, and flickering is active and yang, and is best avoided in bedrooms (even guest bedrooms, if possible). LEDs also flicker and even though it's subtle, it's still there. So that leaves us with incandescent bulbs, which are being improved, and halogen bulbs. One other great reason for not having fluorescent bulbs is that they contain mercury. If a bulb should break in your bedroom, the *first* thing you should do is leave the room so the mercury vapor can settle. You should put on a breathing mask and then open windows so that the toxic vapor can disperse. Yuck! Don't bring that possibility into a room that should be a refuge. Fluorescent bulbs, including compact fluorescents, should be disposed of as toxic waste, because the mercury could eventually find its way into water, and future generations would curse us for spreading this extremely toxic substance.

If a bare bulb is seen, use one that doesn't have a brand name and wattage printed on the round part. The wattage is usually written on the bulb where the metal screw-part begins. If a bare bulb is seen, you shouldn't see the filament. The bare filament is too jarring on the eyes when the bulb is on. Clear bulbs should be used in locations where the bulb isn't seen and the shadows don't look weird. Their best application is often as uplights behind a plant, accenting the natural plant shape on the ceiling and walls. Clear bulbs should never be used around mirrors above a bathroom sink. Do your eyes a favor and use frosted bulbs instead. Silver-tipped bulbs are a perfect choice in the right setting and can dramatically change the atmosphere in the room, because *all* the light is reflected from the wall or ceiling—*none* of the light comes to your eyes directly from the bulb. Not every bedroom needs them, and they should never be used around a bathroom mirror, because that's where you want to be able to have *very* strong light. Dimmers can be useful on bathroom mirrors that are surrounded on three sides by light bulbs. But do be aware of the chances of creating a buzzing sound by installing a dimmer. If you're sensitive to the buzzing sound that accompanies most dimmer applications, you might want to use lower-wattage bulbs instead. It is important to have all the light sockets filled with bulbs, and that every bulb function. Otherwise the message that you're sending is "something doesn't work here."

Halogen ceiling lights (which are often recessed in modern bedrooms) can have a uniquely high electromagnetic field. This is not always the case, but the newer high-end electronically-controlled lighting systems can have a setting for "everything on." When all the halogen downlights (and more) are turned on throughout the house, there might be no place safe in the building from the elevated electromagnetic fields. If you can afford such an electrical system, hopefully you can buy a gaussmeter ($30) and check it yourself.

Chapter 9

The Bagua

A Bagua Map begins as a Yin/Yang
laid down over the room

Fig. 9.1

A bagua (or pakua) is basically a big yin/yang symbol that flops
down over the room. You enter at the yin part of the yin/yang.
It is more complicated than a simple yin/yang because the Five
Elements come into play. The bagua grid overlies the floor
plan of the bedroom. There are nine areas in the room—eight
around the walls, and one in the center. These areas relate to
aspects of a person's life. The bagua is largely based on the eight
I Ching trigrams (see Glossary if you are not familiar with the

I Ching), which identify with the eight areas, or guas, around the center. It is also based on the Five Elements. The areas that most strongly relate to a particular element are the five areas that are not in corners. See Fig. 9.2.

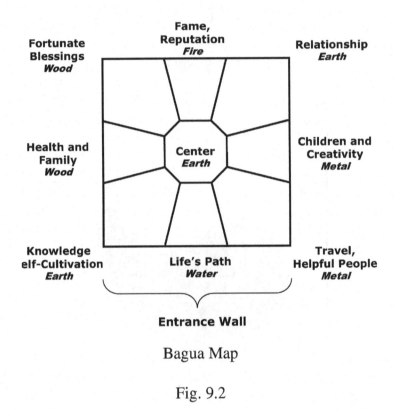

Bagua Map

Fig. 9.2

In Chapter 2, I explained yin and yang in relation to the busyness outside. This has nothing to do with that. The yin/yang of the bagua is primarily about the interior world of the home, and the individual rooms.

A bagua grid can be laid over a room, or over the house as a whole, based on the front door as the entrance. It is most powerful when applied per room, because when you are in a room, that's the space that is affecting you the most at that time—not some distant part of the home. It can be applied to a parcel of land, usually based on the driveway entrance. It can even be applied to a desktop (based on the side you sit on being the entrance), if the desk is used for several hours daily. The bagua is most powerful in spaces where people spend more time.

The Five Elements

According to Taoist teaching, all the manifest energy of the universe can be divided among five archetypal elements—Water, Wood, Fire, Earth, and Metal. There are shapes and colors that signify each individual element.

Water—The shape is wavy or freeform like waves or a river meandering, or a drop that's splashed. The color is black like a deep, dark well. Dark blue also represents Water.

Wood—The shape is square or a vertical rectangle like tree trunks. The color is green like leaves; blue works equally well.

Fire—The shape is any angular shape like a pyramid or cone, symbolizing a flame rising. The color is red, or possibly purple.

Metal—The shape is round, oval, or arched. The color is white. Imagine light glinting off polished metal. That glint is taken to be white. This also includes very light colors such as pastels.

Earth—The shape is square or a horizontal rectangle symbolizing the horizon. The color is yellow or any earth tone such as brown or burnt orange.

Before explaining the nine bagua areas in detail, one more feng shui concept should be explained—the concept of Elemental Cycles. At this point, feng shui can take a major detour into the world of the complicated. The background of knowledge of the elemental cycles can put off some people, but it is a great aid in feng shui. It is particularly useful in working with the individual bagua areas. For instance, if it were desirable to enhance the Fame area, but red colors and fiery symbols were inappropriate for the decor, wood items could be used since wood feeds fire.

Chart of Bagua Areas

Area (Gua)	Alternate Names	Element	Color	Shape
Life's Path	Career The Journey	Water The Most Yin	Black and very dark colors	Freeform
Knowledge	Contemplation Wisdom Meditation Intuition	Earth Neutral	Black, dark green, and dark blue	
Health and Family	Ancestors Elders Community New Beginning	Wood Mostly Yang	Green and blue	Vertical, rectangular, or square
Fortunate Blessings	Wealth Empowerment Intention Abundance	Wood Mostly Yang	Rich shades of purple, blue, and red Also green	
Fame	Reputation Illumination Future Recognition	Fire The Most Yang	Red, maroon, magenta, any shade of red, even including violet & purple	Angular, triangular, pointed, conical, or uprising
Relationship	Love Marriage Partnership Commitment	Earth Neutral	Pink, white, red, and yellow	
Children and Creativity	Descendants Completion Joy Pleasure	Metal Mostly Yin	White and pastels	Circular, oval, or arched
Helpful People and Travel	Benefactors Compassion Determination Persistence	Metal Mostly Yin	Black, white, or gray	
Center	Health Unity Tai Chi Wholeness	Earth Neutral	Yellow and earth tones such as brown, gold, and orange	Horizontal, square, rectangular or octagonal

I Ching trigram	Meaning of Trigram	Comments
	Water	Perfect place for a fountain, or picture of water flowing into the room. Objects made of glass. Items related to your career, but not awards, awards should be in the Fame Area.
	Mountain	Good place for books and learning tools, including television or computer or audio equipment. Images of mountains, but not images of water.
	Thunder	Good place for plants and images of plants. Wooden furniture, especially tall furniture. Pictures of your ancestors, including your parents.
	Wind	Expensive items, things that move or attract attention. No open trashcans. Great place for a fountain or picture of water. Also plants or pictures of plants are good here.
	Fire	Items related to fame such as awards. Things representing animals or made of animals—fur, bone, leather, feathers, etc. Also things made of plastic or that use electricity.
	Earth	Pictures of loved ones, pairs and groupings of things. No outstanding singular objects. Preferably no TV. Make this area look romantic to you.
	Lake	Pictures of children, or items that relate to children, and/or creativity. If you have children, the maintenance of this area could affect them.
	Heaven or Father	Images of deities, angels, holy people, teachers, or mentors—also affirmations. But no feminine images in this area, any angel images should seem masculine.
No trigram		No bathroom, ever! A good place for pottery, perhaps yellow pottery. If possible, try to keep this area open and traversable.

Elemental Cycles

The five elements relate to each other in several dynamic cycles of creation and destruction. The study of these cycles can be daunting to a beginner, and for simplicity I am only including the standard creation and destruction cycles.

In the *creative cycle* each element is considered to give birth to the next element.

Wood	creates	Fire	(wood is the fuel)
Fire	creates	Earth	(ashes are as dirt)
Earth	creates	Metal	(through time and pressure)
Metal	creates	Water	(through condensation)
Water	creates	Wood	(water is essential to plants)

The *destructive cycle* is not the reverse of the creative cycle. The interaction is rearranged, and the result is quite negative.

Wood	destroys	Earth	(plants eat dirt)
Earth	destroys	Water	(the result is mud)
Water	destroys	Fire	(quite obviously)
Fire	destroys	Metal	(through melting)
Metal	destroys	Wood	(axes and saws kill trees)

These cycles can be called upon in deciding what to do when there is too much of an element in the room.

When there is too much:	Add:
Wood	Metal or Fire
Water	Earth or Wood
Metal	Fire or Water
Earth	Wood or Metal
Fire	Water or Earth

Applying the Bagua

To apply the bagua, imagine it enlarged and stretched to fit the bedroom. An example of how a bagua is shaped for a rectangular bedroom is shown in Fig. 9.3.

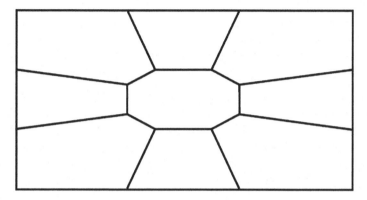

Bagua stretched to fit rectangular shape

Fig. 9.3

There are two equally popular approaches to orienting the bagua. The Form School has one method—using the form of the building. In this approach the door to the room is the key orienting factor. The door is known as the "mouth of chi." We enter through the door, and so does chi. This method of orienting the bagua places the grid so the side that says Water is along the entrance wall. Several sub-schools of feng shui use the entrance to orient the bagua. Some of them are: Eight-point, Black Sect, Intuitive, and Pyramid. None of those names says much about it, so I generally refer to it as "entrance-based bagua" for the sake of clarity.

The other method of orienting the bagua is based on the cardinal directions—north, south, east, west. This type of feng shui relies heavily on Chinese astrology and numerology, and is called Compass School. To use this method, place the side of the grid that says Fire to the south.

People who have read more than one book about feng shui sometimes become quite confused. Unbeknownst to them, they may have read different approaches to orienting the bagua. Most books fail to mention that there is more than one way to do it. Pick one method of orienting the bagua. Use the entrance or use the compass. Stick with that method, or give it a good try for at least six months. If you mix and match the two different methods of orienting the bagua, you will *not* be practicing good feng shui—guaranteed.

This book bases the bagua on the entrance. I have nothing against numerology or astrology. I'm sure they are fine systems, but I do not base my life around them and I do not ask my clients to do so. I am more drawn to arranging furniture and household items beautifully and correctly. If you want Chinese astrology and numerology to play a more active role in your life, read a good book on Compass School feng shui, such as *Practical Feng Shui* by Simon Brown, and orient the bagua with the Fame area to the south.

What follows is a list of the nine guas (or bagua areas) with suggestions for improving or enhancing them.

Life's Path

Water is the element in the center of the entrance wall of the room. It symbolizes movement and has to do with one's journey through life. This is often referred to as the Career area, but it relates to more than just income-earning livelihood. When water is moving it is responding to a natural law—gravity. It is very powerful to put a picture of flowing water in this area—a picture of a stream, river, or gentle waterfall. A major waterfall such as Niagara or Victoria Falls is a bit too powerful. If such a picture were in the Life's Path area it would be like asking for a stampede in your life. It is not ideal to put a picture of still or stagnant water here, such as a lake, pond, or the ocean. The ocean is not considered to be going anywhere—just sloshing back and forth. By representing *flowing water* in the Life's Path area, you are setting up a dynamic in your own life to keep yourself on track with your life's purpose.

Black is the ideal color in this area, but if that just isn't you, use dark blue or whatever dark tones appeal to you. Even dark furniture will do. Items made of glass are good to use here, especially if they have a freeform, watery look. In fact, any freeform, amorphous-shaped objects are appropriate here. Mirrors also represent water. Water features such as a fountain are a possibility, keeping in mind the cautions about fountains in bedrooms in Chapter 7.

If you are making a career change, be sure this area stays clutter-free to allow fresh energy to flow in easily. Items that have to do with your career are appropriate in this area.

Knowledge and Self-Cultivation

Wisdom, Meditation, and Contemplation are other names for this area. The *I Ching* trigram for this area is Mountain, and it is a great place to put pictures of mountains, representing a mountain of knowledge. It is also a good place for images of deities, spiritual teachers, and wise people. It is an excellent area for an altar. It would be best to leave out images of water because the element that is associated with this area is Earth. When earth and water mix the result is mud. Black, blue, and green are the ideal colors, but the blue and green should preferably be dark tones. Books, stereos, and other learning tools are appropriate here, including televisions and computers. Such things are questionable in a bedroom, but sometimes there is no other place for them in the home.

Health and Family

The family that this area refers to is your ancestors—your parents and those who came before them. If you want pictures of those people in your bedroom (many people don't), put them in this area. They are able to offer more resonance in your life from this gua. That this area also represents health is appropriate because our genes can predispose us to certain health conditions or immunities.

Wood is the element here and plants are perfect in the Health/Family area, especially trees such as ficus or palms. Representations of plants are also good—any pictures of healthy growing plants, especially trees. Wooden furniture is ideal here. Metal furniture is not so ideal, metal implements being a major destroyer of living trees. Items that represent fire, such as candles, angular objects, red things, and fireplaces should not be in this area, or they should be kept to a minimum here. If there is a fireplace in this area it can portend health problems such as fatigue. De-emphasize the fireplace by using an opaque screen. Items that represent Water or Earth are good here because that's what plants need to grow.

The shape for Wood is rectangular, like tall growing trees. Square is also good. Tall wooden furniture (such as shelving, a cabinet, or an armoire) is perfect to use in this area. The best colors are green and/or blue.

Fortunate Blessings

This area is commonly called the Wealth Corner—and for good reason. It represents prosperity in its many forms, including, of course, money. Other names for this area are Intention and Empowerment. It is a powerful area, and improvements here are like waving a red flag to the Universe.

One of the basic things to know about this area is that it must be clean, uncluttered, and well maintained. If anything in this area is broken, either fix it or move it. If anything in this area is useless, get rid of it. It is great to have plants here (the bigger the better), but they must be healthy, look vibrant, and have no thorns or sharp pointy leaves.

As you might imagine, the Wealth area is an ideal place to put expensive things—things that were a stretch for you to afford. Paying more than you had budgeted for an object in the Fortunate Blessings area gives you what I call "the ouch factor." It hurt your pocketbook. The symbolism of its being an expensive object is present in your life. The money you spent for it will come back to you many times over. The Wealth Corner is a great place to keep money, but not fake money, and not small change.

Royal purple is an ideal color here, as well as cobalt blue, and bold Chinese red. Green can also be a good color here because Wood is the element that is associated with this area. Gold also works because it indicates wealth and represents Earth, which feeds Wood. Use rich, vibrant, saturated colors, and if the colors are appropriately brilliant, you don't always have to use a lot to be effective. You probably shouldn't try to use all the colors here. The result would probably be quite hodge-podge. This area should look nice (if not gorgeous).

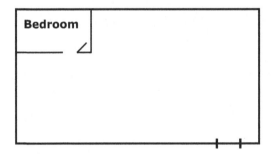

Bedroom in the Fortunate Blessings area

Fig. 9.4

I once had a single client whose bedroom Wealth Corner was also the Wealth Corner of the whole house. See Fig. 9.4. I suggested red or purple for the back wall of the bedroom. She chose purple and here's the email she sent me a few years later:

"You came to our house to do a consult right after we moved in and suggested that I paint a wall in my bedroom red or purple—it was the wealth corner of the house and also the wall that connected the wealth and relationship corners in my room.

"Well, I painted the wall a deep, vibrant purple and a number of things happened:

—We sold the house for almost 3 times what we paid for it, and I received ten times my cash investment (the next month the real estate market froze)

—I became romantically involved with a friend (unplanned, unexpected, and fabulous)."

Her son-in-law (who was also living there) received a tremendously good job offer at the same time.

Fountains are absolutely perfect in the Fortunate Blessings Area. But since it's a bedroom, see the cautions under Fountains in Chapter 7. Prismatic crystals are great here and so are wind chimes. Mirrors are not great here because they represent windows and they are an opportunity for chi to leak away. Trash cans should not be in this corner of the room. That says that you are throwing your money away. If, for some reason, the trash can must be in this corner, it should have a lid so chi energy doesn't find it. As one client commented, "It's pretty easy to fool chi energy."

Fame

This area has to do with your reputation and the future, and with what people are saying about you. Fire is the element here, and is represented by red, ideally a very brilliant primary red. Such a saturated color is not always appropriate to add to a bedroom. However, if you need fame in your work, I advise you to learn to love this color. Thousands of dollars of publicity will not buy what the bold use of candy-apple red can achieve if used in the Fame area. If you need fame, you cannot overdo it. If you just want a good reputation you certainly can tone it down. Maroon, old rose, magenta, basically any color that is in the warm end of the spectrum will have a good effect. Dusty rose is often the best choice for a bedroom. If it is a relationship bedroom, the warm color will say that there is a warm relationship. A red with a lot of orange in it such as terra cotta is not recommended in the Fame area, because it represents Earth.

The shape for Fire is pointed, like a flame rising up. Cones, pyramids and triangles are appropriate, as well as any shape that is sharply angular. Examples are red tapered candles or a picture of buildings with red, pointed roofs. A fireplace is auspicious in this area, if it is actually used. It is the one area where I most definitely do not recommend water features (such as fountains) or representations of water (such as ocean pictures). This area is perfect for hanging diplomas or awards, especially with red frames or red matting.

Animals are considered to have the spark of life within them, so items of animal origin are appropriate here. Such things might be made of leather, feathers, bone, horn, or fur. Pictures or figurines of animals are also good. Avoid things that come from or represent water animals in this area, such as seashells or sand dollars or pictures of fish or sea mammals.

Relationship

The Relationship area doesn't concern just romantic relationships. It concerns relationships of all kinds: friends, co-workers, et cetera. The most important thing to note about this area is that there should not be any outstanding singular objects here. If there is a pole lamp, it should be supported by more than one pole, or have more than one bulb. It is best if things in this area relate to each other. There is a design concept that things are either in conflict or in conversation. In this area, they need to be in conversation. As for pictures, it would be best if they were in pairs or groupings. If there is only one picture, it should have several items within it, such as a group of flowers, or a couple of people. Don't have pictures of your ex-sweetheart here. They can hold you back from finding the right person. If you are looking for a new relationship, you should be free of any previous personal relationship, both legally and visually! Wedding pictures on display do not help to bind a relationship together. Those photographs are of a moment in time, while your on-going relationship is based on who you are *now* and how you're treating your partner *now*. *Your* wedding pictures are best in an album, but wedding pictures of your ancestors are fine to have in the Relationship corner (or in the Health and Family area). The Relationship corner is an ideal place to put a grouping of almost anything. However, things that might represent conflict, such as guns or swords, should never be kept in the Relationship area or anywhere on display in a bedroom.

If a desk is in a Relationship area, certain innocent desk items should not be on display. Anything that could conceivably cut or hurt someone should be stored out of sight. Put scissors in a drawer, and also put away the stapler, staple remover, tape dispenser, and letter opener. If the desk is not in the relationship area of the room, it doesn't matter if those items are on view.

Be careful about the cutting items. They shouldn't be in the far right corner of any desk, no matter where it is in the room. That is the relationship area of the desk. More information on applying the bagua to a desk is in Chapter 13.

This area especially concerns women and feminine energy. Pink is the ideal color here. Red, white, and yellow also work. Dusty rose counts as pink, and goes well in many decors. Avoid fabric with stripes (considered to represent conflict) in this area.

Things that have a romantic association are appropriate here—hearts and flowers, if that's your style. Televisions are not so appropriate. They can signify a life in which the television is the main relationship. If there is no other place to have the television, it is best to cover it when it is not in use. It is also good to have something higher than the television, such as pictures, above it on the wall. Higher says "more important." Telephones are fine in the Relationship area, and so are computers. Computers are used for two-way communication—televisions are not.

Children and Creativity

If you have children, this area will always affect them, even if they have moved away. It will also affect your grandchildren and beyond. Here is a great place to put pictures or mementos of your children or grandchildren. If you don't have children, this area is about your ideas and creativity. They are what you leave behind when you die. Metal is the element here and is represented by white or pastels. Objects that have a metallic finish are also appropriate. The shape for Metal is round, with oval or arched being equally good. Creativity is associated with this element, and the rounded shapes help ideas flow. Some objects that would be very appropriate here are: round mirrors, round baskets, pictures with round matting or frames, round metal plates or trays, and round metal lamps or pole lights.

Helpful People and Travel

Heaven is the *I Ching* trigram for this area. People who help you can be thought of as heaven sent. This area of the room is a great place to put pictures of people who have been helpful to you, such as mentors, teachers, and benefactors—although not necessarily relatives. Images of deities or holy people would also be appropriate here, as well as angels or guardian beings. It is the masculine area of the bagua so any angel images here should not look feminine.

If you would like to travel more, put a picture here of someplace far away, perhaps a picture of someplace that you've been or where you'd like to visit. Also any items that have come from other lands would be good to put here. Choose items that are obviously from far away.

This is an area for neutral tones—white, black, or gray. This area especially affects men, and masculine energy.

Center

This area concerns health, and people's ability to integrate all of who they are into a healthy personality. It is the only gua that touches all the other guas. Earth is represented by yellow or any earth tones such as ochre or brown. The shape is square or a horizontal rectangle. Pottery and beautiful sand are ways to bring real earth into this area. Representations of water are not recommended in the Center because the element is Earth, and when water and earth are mixed, the result is mud.

In ancient China (and many other cultures), the center of a house was often an open-air courtyard. Here one walked across actual earth to reach the various areas of the house. The healthiest living spaces I have seen are those in which the center (of the room, house, or apartment) is open and uncluttered. This is hardly feasible in a small bedroom where the bed takes up most of the space. In that case, just try to have Earth represented by color or shape—for example a brown or yellow blanket at the foot of the bed.

Chapter 10

The Shape of the Bedroom

Most bedrooms are rectangular or square, with flat ceilings. Great! That's ideal in feng shui. If that is what you have, you can skip this chapter. But if the floor plan of the bedroom is not a perfect square or rectangle, or if the ceiling is sloped, please read on.

Brick Walls and Split Views

A "brick wall" is the feng shui term for a wall that causes you to change direction just as soon as you've walked into a room. A brick wall causes the bagua of the room to shift so that the entrance wall is determined by the direction you are facing after you have turned to the right or left as you walk on into the room, as in Fig. 10.1.

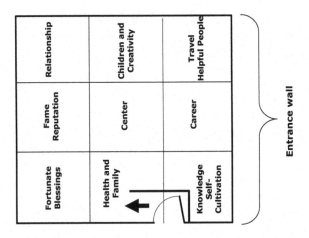

Brick Wall with Bagua based on turn

Fig. 10.1

A split view is similar, except that the wall in front of you doesn't extend as far, and the bagua is still based on the actual door. It is as if one eye sees the wall and the other eye sees on into the room, as in Fig. 10.2.

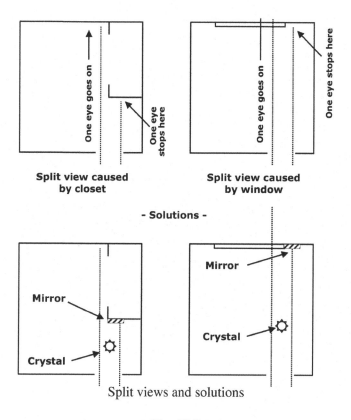

Split views and solutions

Fig. 10.2

Both are fairly common in bedrooms and are often caused by closets.

The main problem caused by brick walls and split views is not related to the bagua. It has to do with the symbolism of the architectural feature. A brick wall symbolizes, "I was intending to go forward, but now I have to change plans." A split view symbolizes disagreement— "I see things one way and you see things another way." For a person living alone, this can manifest in difficulty in making up one's mind.

The solutions to both problems are exactly the same. Hang a clear, disco-ball shaped crystal between the door and the wall, saying, "This symbolizes that the energy that's coming into the room is dispersed before it meets the brick wall (or split view)." Use any words to that effect. The other solution is to put a mirror on the wall, which symbolizes that the wall has been erased, and you should say so out loud at the time of putting up the mirror. The mirror can be any size, from full-length to dime-size. A small mirror can be hidden behind a picture. The best picture to put on the wall is one that shows perspective, as if you could keep on walking into the scene in the picture.

Extensions and Missing Areas

Any deviation from a perfect square or rectangle should be thought of as either an extension or a missing area. Extensions such as bay windows are generally to your benefit, but missing areas present a problem. They indicate a "lack" in that bagua area.

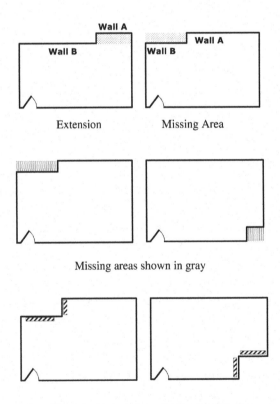

Extension   Missing Area

Missing areas shown in gray

Locations of mirrors to bring back a missing area

Fig. 10.3

There are several methods for determining whether an irregular room has an extension or a missing area. Sometimes it is obvious by simply looking. The lengths of the pieces of the broken wall (made up of walls A and B in Fig. 10.3) are compared. If the part of the wall that is farthest from the heart of the room (wall A in Example 1) is longer, then there is a missing area outside the room. The gray areas in Examples 1, 3, & 4 are missing areas. If the wall that is farthest from the heart of the room (wall A in Example 2) is shorter than wall B, then there is an extension. The gray area in Example 2 is an extension with wall A as the outermost wall of the extension.

There are various other methods for mathematically figuring whether rooms have missing areas or extensions. Different teachers usually have a particular method that they prefer. Use the method that feels right to you. Also use your intuition, experience, and a keen eye, noting such things as whether the floor or ceiling changes in the vicinity of the missing area or extension. Such a change often signals an extension. Anything that says "add-on" is usually an extension.

Bringing Back a Missing Area

If an area is missing from a room, it needs to be symbolically brought back. Do so by placing a mirror on wall 1 and wall 2 as indicated in Fig. 10.3. The mirrors should face into the bedroom. When bringing back a missing area, the mirror (or mirrors) should be as large as possible. That can present a problem in bedrooms, where many people prefer to keep mirrors to a minimum. If you prefer to keep mirrors to a minimum in the bedroom, but need to bring back a missing area, then consider placing them high on the wall, above head height. This is not appropriate in all decors. If it works in your decor, it will work even better if the mirror reflects something interesting or lovely. If it reflects something that is attention-getting, it will be more effective because the interesting object will be seen twice, and the reflection will appear to be inside the missing area. If you don't mind an excess of mirrors in the bedroom (see cautions under Mirrors in Chapter 7) feel free to mirror walls 1 and 2 completely, but don't use mirror tiles (because they slice up your image). The visual effect is that the room actually extends into a corner. This causes the room to seem more like a square or rectangle.

You do not have to use that much mirror to be effective, and in a bedroom especially, it's good to have less mirror surface. You can simply place a small mirror on wall 1 or wall 2. It does not have to be on both walls, and it does not have to be a large mirror. The mirror serves as a window into another room. If you were Alice (as in *Alice Through the Looking Glass*) you could actually go into that room. You would still be in the same bedroom, because that is what the mirror is showing.

Atul Gawande's perceptive article, *The Itch*, from *The New Yorker* (June 30, 2008) reveals in detail how mirrors fool our brain into perceiving a different reality—in this case, an expanded reality. Gawande says, "perception is the brain's best guess about what is happening in the outside world." Later he says, "Perception is inference." I highly recommend the article to understand why mirrors are important in feng shui. Special mirror boxes are now being used by patients who have lost a limb and consequently have "phantom limb" pain. The recoveries are often instant—just by using mirrors!

If you want mirrors to be kept to an absolute minimum in the bedroom, then use the tiny ones that are sold in craft stores. Some are smaller than a dime. The small mirror does not have to be seen. It can be placed behind a picture or furniture. This is the type of solution that most people use. No matter what size mirror is being used, this solution is symbolic, and requires that you say out loud why you are placing the mirror—to bring back a missing area.

Mirrors are the most common way of bringing back a missing area—but if there is a window on one of the walls that has a mirror in the lower examples of Fig. 10.3, perhaps it would work to have a windowbox or birdfeeder just outside the window. A silent wind catcher placed outside the window is also helpful. You are thereby claiming occupancy of the missing area by using some of it.

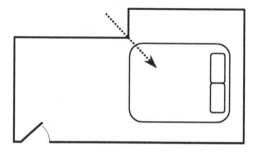

Poison arrow caused by a corner

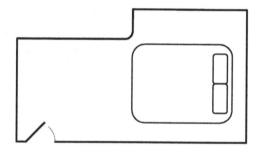

Bullnose corner eliminates Poison Arrow
Fig. 10.4

An irregularly shaped bedroom often has a poison arrow that originates from a corner that juts into the room. If the poison arrow goes across the bed, as in Fig. 10.4, something must be done. If you own the home, I suggest that you bullnose (see Glossary) the corner and forget about it. A rounded corner does not cause a poison arrow. If that isn't feasible, perhaps three-quarter-round molding could be glued onto the corner, and painted to match the wall. The three-quarter-round could be easily removed if and when you move. Some hardware stores and catalogs sell corner protectors that work the same as the molding. Another option is to make a long, narrow (two or three inches wide) banner hanging from a small dowel and covering the corner. Such fabric banners are easy to make and especially lovely if made of silk. If the bedroom is large enough, the poison arrow can be blunted by putting a plant or piece of furniture at the offending corner. Photo 4.1 shows poison arrows coming from a structural column that juts out from the corner of the room. The open headboard in that picture does nothing to protect the sleeper's body from those poison arrows.

Bedrooms with Sloped Ceilings

There is an energetic imbalance if the bedroom ceiling slopes. There is a pressurized "crunch" of chi energy at the low end of the room. The solutions to this problem are in the ceiling section of Chapter 3. Watch out for exposed beams in bedrooms with sloped ceilings. Bedrooms in the upper part of an A-frame building (where you look up at a peak in the room) *and where the walls are also sloped* are a severe problem. Put up fabric so the ceiling of the bedroom looks level. Any kind of fake ceiling is fine as long as it's level. I can't recommend A-frames, period, except as temporary lodging.

Coffered ceilings have become more common in master bedrooms. The problem is when the bed is partly under the higher part and partly under the lower part of the ceiling. Use an uplight under the lower part of the ceiling. The energy of the light bulb is symbolically lifting the ceiling. A pointed light bulb is ideal in this situation. You could also put a small mirror somewhere under the lower part of the ceiling, with the reflective side shining up. It is symbolically reflecting the ceiling away from the bed and pushing it up.

I've seen some bedrooms that were utterly weird—odd walls, odd ceiling, odd everything. If that's your case, make it the very best you possibly can, and before too long the universe will probably bounce you into a much nicer situation. Bloom where you're planted—and don't be surprised if you get transplanted to someplace nicer.

Chapter 11

Closets

I am occasionally asked whether a closet is an extension of the bagua of the bedroom. Yes and no. Yes, when the door is open; no, when it is closed. Closet doors should not be left open on a regular basis, so generally a closet is not an extension. It is its own separate space, but it is too small a room for the application of a separate bagua. It does *somewhat* influence the bagua area of the bedroom which has the closet door.

The first thing to note about a closet is its door.

Types of Closet Doors

Hinged

The hinges of the closet door (as well as any door in the home) must not squeak. If they do, just use some general household oil on them. Squeaky hinges are considered to portend joint problems.

The knob of the closet door must not be able to swing open and actually touch the knob of another door. If this situation exists, use the red ribbons (or red tassels) that are described in Chapter 7. You can also take the closet door off and put up curtains, if that works aesthetically.

Sliding

If the closet has sliding doors, they should work easily and well. If sliding doors repeatedly come off their tracks, it is adding to the frustration level in your life. Fix them, or hire someone to fix them, or remove them and put up curtains. If you must delay any repair needed on the door, put a small red dot on the back of the door near the problem area. It's a symbolic solution, generally used when you have to live with a broken object, but you don't want the "broken" vibration to be affecting your life. The red symbolizes a new-blood change—a totally new situation. Say out loud when you put the red dot on, "You are not broken. You are fixed," or words to that effect.

Curtains

Curtains work fine as closet doors. They give the opportunity to bring in the correct bagua color by the choice of fabric. If the closet is on the entrance wall, generally use a darker shade of fabric. If the closet door is on the far side of the bedroom (from the entrance) use a bolder and warmer color. See the color bagua map on the back cover. One of my clients took down her sliding closet doors and installed an extension rod at the uppermost part of where the doors had been. She put curtain-holding clips onto the rod. These designer clips resemble shower curtain rings, but they are smaller, and they clip onto whatever fabric is to be the curtain. She had nice curtains with very little work.

Unless a fabric is shiny like metal, it brings a yin quality with it because of its soft flowing nature. Yin is almost always appreciated in a bedroom. Thick, soft fabrics such as velvet are very yin, and quite desirable in most bedrooms.

Mirrored

Some closet doors are mirrored on the outside. It is widely believed in feng shui that mirrors in the bedroom are problematic.

But as with most things in life, some people teach the opposite. Steven Post makes a great case *for* bedroom mirrors in *The Modern Book of Feng Shui*. See Recommended Reading. If you don't have any intuitive or design problems with mirrored closet doors, they may be fine for you. I say, "Judge by how you sleep." You might try covering the doors with fabric for a few weeks, to see if you sleep more soundly. If you sleep just the same, then I doubt that the mirrors are affecting you. Mirrored closet doors tend to affect light sleepers most strongly.

If you decide to cover mirrored doors in a bedroom, put up a sturdy rod and hang curtains. The curtains can be very lightweight. I have also seen mirrored closet doors that were thoroughly painted over in the same color as the bedroom walls, and the effect was very peaceful.

Organization of Closets

The organization inside a closet is quite important. Do not store items that you no longer want or use. In *Wind and Water* (see Recommended Reading) Carol Hyder says, "When a closet is jammed full of stuff, the metaphor is that somewhere in your life there's a stagnation and a stuck place that isn't getting loosened. Unload the closet and you'll loosen some aspect of your life."

Color of Hangers

Consider having some or all the clothes hangers of a matching color. The color of the hangers should be the correct bagua color for whichever bagua area(s) within the room the closet door or doors are in.

You can also choose to enhance a particular area of the bagua of your *entire* home (based on the front door), look for any closets that fall within that area. Choose one color for all the bagua hangers in that closet, based on the area of the bagua map they are in, within your home as a whole. The color of the hangers can be based on the color of the bagua, but you have two (possibly different) bagua orientations to choose from. The bagua of your bedroom (based on the door to the bedroom), or the bagua of the home as a whole (based on the front door). If you spend a large amount of time in the bedroom, I recommend emphasizing the area for the bagua of the *room*. If you live in a medium-sized or large home and can pick colors of hangers for several closets, base the color selection on the larger bagua which overlies the *entire* home. If it is someone else's bedroom, you might suggest to them the appropriate color for their hangers, based on their bedrooms' location in the entire home.

Direction of Shoes

Our shoes are below us and they symbolize our foundation. When shoes are stored in an area of the closet they should all face the same direction. That way you are not going against yourself. Shoes on one side of the closet do not have to face the same direction as shoes on the opposite side of the closet.

Chapter 12

Children's Rooms

Children are very important people. Apply the same feng shui principles to your children's rooms as you do to the rest of the home. Children's rooms are extremely important to them and to their development. They do present special feng shui challenges, such as being overly busy.

If you have children living at home, I suggest that you give each of them a bagua map to keep, and explain some principles appropriate to their age and comprehension level. If they have their own rooms, be sure to note things such as an open trashcan in a Fortunate Blessings area. Point out what seems appropriate for each child.

A child's room should be neat and clean. If children do not learn cleaning and organizing skills at home, they may never learn them. I recommend that children's allowances be partially based on bedroom maintenance. They may not appreciate the discipline at the moment. They will, however, be grateful the rest of their lives as they reap the benefits of good maintenance, and their future partner will love them more. When they are old enough, let them read *Speed Cleaning* and listen to *Getting Organized*. (See Recommended Reading.)

The door to a child's room should not be directly across the hall from the door to the parent's bedroom. If the doors do directly face each other it represents the child challenging the parent's authority. In that case, hang a crystal in the hall between the two doors to symbolize that the challenging energy is dispersed.

Location of Children's Rooms

When considering the bagua of the house as a whole, a child's bedroom should not be in the Fortunate Blessings area, as in Fig. 9.4. This sets up a dynamic that the child will run the house. If there is no alternative to having a child's bedroom there, a picture of the parents (or head of the household) should be on display in that room—preferably framed and hung on a wall. This reinstates the parent to a place of empowerment.

If a child's bedroom extends beyond the main body of the house, that child may not feel connected to the rest of the family. This situation and its solution are shown in Fig. 2.2 in Chapter 2.

If possible, let children's rooms have a view of nature. A year in a child's life seems longer to the child, because for a five-year-old, one year is one fifth (20%) of their whole life up to that point. For a person who is fifty, one year is only one fiftieth (2%) of their life. Seeing nature will teach them to love nature—it's the best antidote to "screen time" during those long, formative years. It beckons the child to participate in nature and fresh air.

For academic improvement, have children's rooms in quiet parts of the home and insist that their sleep begin well before midnight. Scientific studies have linked poor sleep patterns to poor academic performance. A Columbia University study found that teenagers whose parents allowed a midnight or later bedtime were much more likely to suffer from depression and have suicidal thoughts.

Colors

Feng shui consultants often recommend green for children's bedrooms. It represents Wood and signifies growth. Blue and yellow are also recommended. The yellow should be toned down, like mustard, not bright lemon yellow. Beige, off-white, and very light pink are also fine. The main colors in the room should not be overly bold and vivid. Children can find enough stimulation in life without their room colors' screaming at them. However, the room colors should not be *too* somber. It is fine to have brilliant colors, but use them as accents. If a child is overactive, steer away from reds, especially primary red.

Some teenagers want an abundance of black in their room. Black absorbs all other colors, and can represent learning and introspection. If your teenager wants to paint the room black, I suggest making an agreement with them. They must do the job themselves, do it to your standards, and agree to bring it to white when it's time to move out. It will take multiple coats both times. They will have learned valuable painting skills, including prep and cleanup. If you don't want that much black in a bedroom, consider a compromise where just the entrance wall is black. If you are dead set against seeing black in a bedroom, but the teen really wants it, consider black sheets. They are restful, easily available, and you won't usually see them. Another way to compromise on this color issue is to use gray.

If children are sad or depressed, do not let there be an over abundance of blue in their bedroom—that would say, "I have the blues." Too much gray could also be a problem, like "I'm under a dark cloud." If gray is used in a child's room, it should be a warm gray, which will have a slight hint of green.

Children's favorite colors often change over time. The favorite colors of children (under the age of eight) are red, yellow, and white. Cooler colors, blues and greens, are preferred by people over the age of eight. (This is according to polls conducted in the United States, Canada, and Western Europe.) So even if red is your child's favorite color, don't use the paintbrush, because the child will probably outgrow it; and even if blue is your child's favorite color, don't overdo it. You can't overdo white, as long as it's a somewhat off-white. Green and yellow are also colors that can be used in abundance.

Beds

While I rarely recommend that an adult bed have the long side against a wall, that is okay for a child's bed. In small bedrooms, it allows for more play space. If children share a bedroom, try to have the beds facing the same direction. It brings more harmony. Also do not hang mobiles or other objects directly over a child's bed. Your baby will develop just fine without a mobile looming over them. Sheets and bedding with very busy patterns (sports, cartoons, action figures) are not as restful as plain solid colors. Consider using sheets that are the child's favorite color, but not bright red.

Bunk beds should only be used if there is absolutely no alternative. Trundle beds do not usually present a feng shui problem. More information on bunks and trundles is in Chapter 4.

Televisions and Computers

A child or teenager's room is often more than just a place to sleep. For many young people, their bedroom is also a big slice of their world. There should never be an actual television in a child's room—period. A television in a child's bedroom has been proven to lower the child's IQ. Children will, in the future, need every bit of intelligence they can get. The eloquent author Guy Davenport puts it in well in his essay *On Reading*, "television idiotizes and blinds while reading makes for intelligence and perception." If there is a computer in a child's room, make very sure that the child does not become a screen junkie at an early age. Proper human development requires the use and exercise of all muscles. People who are hooked on television or computers benefit from regular swimming and exercise that also develops social skills. Parents who show educational videos to babies and toddlers should know that the main thing they are doing is addicting those children to screens. Studies have shown that the babies learn practically nothing that way. However, the same studies show that those young children learn readily when taught the old fashioned way, with direct human interaction.

John Rosemond is a family psychologist and columnist. Here's what he says: "Don't allow televisions, video game consoles, or computers in your children's rooms, and restrict total screen time to no more than one hour per day. As screen time has increased for America's kids, so has their weight."

Other Objects

If any dolls or plush animals are visible in the room, they may be adding to a "stay awake" vibration if they can't close their eyes. Dolls, action figures, and plush animals can be considered to be awake all the time if their eyes can't close. Cover them at night in a cupboard or behind a nice cloth. Not everyone is very sensitive to the stay awake vibration. Judge by how soundly the child generally sleeps. It's certainly all right for the child to take a soft toy to bed with them.

Action figure and music celebrity pictures are going to go up on the walls in some children's bedrooms or else the parent may be seen as a tyrant. Younger children should not be encouraged to put up posters, but once they're teenagers any perky posters should be allowed within reason. The posters must be perky and not sinister or depressing. It's your home—you get to veto any sinister posters that go up. Sinister posters aren't good for anyone. That's just common sense.

Any pictures of your children that are on display in their bedroom (or anywhere in the home) should be fairly current, if the children are teenage or younger. Young children are growing and developing rapidly. It doesn't help them to repeatedly see images of themselves when they were less developed, such as an infant on a bearskin rug picture.

If the child has or wants an aquarium, it would be best to keep it out of the bedroom. If it must be in the child's bedroom, try to have it in the Fortunate Blessings or Life's Path area of the room. Do not have it near the head of the bed because it is a fairly active object with bubbles, lights, and moving fish, as well as high EMFs when the pump is on.

I can't imagine a child's room without books. Just be sure that there aren't too many books close to the head of the bed or under the bed. Also, don't let the bookshelves send a poison arrow or any cutting energy toward the bed. See Bookshelves, in Chapter 6.

Chapter 13

Studio Apartments

A studio apartment can be a feng shui powerhouse because the occupant lives primarily in one room. Remember, the more time you spend in a particular room, the more the energy of that space affects you. But the various functions of a studio are often at odds with one another—the busyness of a desk or work area versus the restfulness of a bed.

Studio apartments consist of one main room, plus a bathroom and often, a separate kitchen. The main room is an everything room: living room, bedroom, study, and dining room. Efficiency studios even have the kitchen along one wall. It's best to separate different use areas, and this is not feasible in most studio apartments. The limitations of space just don't permit it. Folding screens are wonderful in studios, if there is adequate space. They provide the needed separation between different use areas. It is especially important that the bed be screened from a desk or work area.

Furniture on wheels is very popular and works great in modern interiors. The wheels on this kind of furniture can be rather large, and make for quick, easy moving. Furniture that moves quickly out of the way when necessary can be a pleasure to live with it a studio apartment, but make sure that it feels quite stable when it's not moving. Furniture on wheels always has a yang quality because it can move and is therefore more active. Big wheels are quite yang. Small wheels are almost yin by comparison.

In an ideal studio apartment, the bed disappears when it is not being slept on. A Murphy bed is an example of this. Second best would be a bed that is folded into a couch during the day. If the bed must remain in view during the day, try to provide adequate chairs so that the bed is seldom used for seating. Of course, in a very small studio the bed often is the only couch. As mentioned in Chapter 5, this is the time to bring on the decorative pillows—any amount, any size; make it like a fancy daybed. Then remove the extra pillows at bedtime. Their purpose is to define the bed as a couch when they're on, and as a bed when they're removed. Add any other decorative fabric throw that appeals to you (such as a bed scarf or afghan). The color and shape of the pillows can emphasize the correct element for their placement in the room. For instance, if the bed is in the Children and Creativity gua, try round white pillows with silver metallic threads in a brocade fabric. In that same gua you could also use shisha embroidery, which is from India and has small round mirrors stitched onto the fabric.

Desk Work

When there is no desk in the studio, desk work is often done at a dining table or coffee table. If this is the case, be sure to clear away the desk work when done. Left out, it will likely be the beginning of a pileup of clutter. As the desk work is put away, the table resumes its original function and serenity reigns in the room.

If there is a desk in the studio, make sure you can see the entrance door when you're working. Use a mirror if necessary. It is fine to leave standard desk items in view such as a pen and pencil holder or letter tray. But try not to leave paperwork in progress in view all the time. A desk such as that is calling you to come and finish the project. We don't need our furniture to be talking to us, especially in the room where we sleep. If a computer is used, try to have a laptop that can be easily closed and put away. If the monitor is stationary, cover it and the keyboard with fabric when it's not in use, and especially when you sleep.

Because of the concentrated work done on a desk surface, it can have a bagua grid applied to it. The entrance side is at the desk chair. The Fortunate Blessings area is the far left corner when you are seated. Appropriate things to put there are: A computer (it's expensive), a vase of flowers or a living plant, an elegant paperweight, or any desk items that are blue, purple, or red. Do not let this area become cluttered or messy. Refer to the principles in Chapter 9 to enhance any other bagua areas of the desk. Be sure not to keep things that could cut (scissors, stapler, staple remover, tape dispenser, or letter opener) in the Relationship area of the desk. A more subtle way to enhance the bagua areas of the desk is by taping colored paper under the desktop. The paper can be cut to the shape of the element for the specific gua. Examples are a red triangle for the Fame area or a foil circle for the Children and Creativity area. The paper cutouts would look quite funky on the desktop, but underneath, no one will see them. You know they're there because you put them there. They're working for you.

Other Considerations

Clutter is a hazard in any bedroom. In a studio apartment it is a severe liability. It is causing chaos and stagnation in the resident's life. Clutter is a self-imposed problem. Reread the section on Clutter in Chapter 7, and take it to heart. If you live in a studio apartment, you must restrict the number of things that you own. The items that surround you can be beautiful, but first they should be functional.

A fountain may not seem functional, but if it's in the Fortunate Blessings area of the apartment, it will be functioning for you. You will probably want to turn it off at night. Use a timer if that's more convenient.

If you can place a doormat outside your studio apartment, do so. Make sure that it has some red or even is completely red. It will be acting as a stop sign to chi energy. "Stop! Come in here." A red tassel on your outside doorknob will do the same thing.

If you live in a studio apartment, don't stay cooped up in that one room. Your bright spirit appreciates large doses of nature to stay bright. Get outside and into nature.

Chapter 14

Guestrooms and Other Special Bedrooms

Guestrooms

A guestroom is quite handy, but if it is used infrequently, it can impart a stagnant energy to the home. Check the bagua for the entire home to see what aspect of your life corresponds to that room. The most problematic area for a guestroom is the Fortunate Blessings corner. It gives the guests too much power in the household, it's a problem if they don't keep the room neat, and it can even be a problem when no one is visiting. The Fortunate Blessings area of the home should never feel stagnant. It should seem alive and vibrant.

Don't try to apply the bagua to the individual space of a guestroom. It's not used by the same person enough for that application of the bagua to matter. Instead, see where the guestroom is in the bagua of the whole home, and enhance it based on that larger bagua. You can enhance it with items listed in the Chart of Bagua Areas in Chapter 9.

Any guestroom benefits from enhancements that liven it up. Such things could include a faceted lead crystal, especially in a window that receives direct sunlight, a wind chime, especially near a window that is occasionally opened for fresh air, or a small decorative light that comes on for a few hours each evening. It is especially good if the light is visible to someone passing by the room. You can also use a fountain that runs all the time. It is fine for guests to turn the fountain off when they are staying there. The easiest way to do this is by installing an on/off switch that the fountain plugs into.

If possible, keep the guestroom door open when no one is staying there. A closed-up room always says "stagnant." A guestroom is, of course, less stagnant if it is a multipurpose room—doubling as an office or a workroom. If the guestroom also functions as an office, cover any monitor screens while guests are there. Laptops with their closeable screens are ideal.

If there is no separate guestroom and the guests must sleep on a sofa bed in a more public room, be considerate of their needs. Try to provide ample closet, cabinet, or drawer space so they don't have to leave their things in view. If household members need to pass through the room while guests are there, use folding screens (or something similar) to partition off a more private area. Three of the nicest things that you can provide a guest are: natural bedding, quiet, and (weather permitting) a bit of natural air circulation.

If your guests have a separate bathroom, it's fine to provide a fresh bar of soap, but be sure to unwrap it—otherwise it's too "hotel-like."

When you are a guest in someone's home, be aware of poison arrows that aim across the bed. Cover them when going to bed, but remove the coverings when you arise. That way you won't inadvertently cause your host to feel uncomfortable or think of your behavior as strange and ungrateful. When you return home, send the host a thank you note to show your appreciation.

We are all guests on planet Earth. In the same sense, you are a guest in the home that shelters you. Be grateful for your home and your bedroom. Occasionally say to your bedroom that you appreciate it and are grateful to it. This is not a silly thing to do. Rather, it is a verbal expression of what should be a constant attitude of gratitude. Both you and your bedroom will benefit from the expression.

Hotel Rooms

When staying in public lodging, ask for a room in the rear half of the building and away from the elevator. If any of the furniture (side tables or dressers, for example) aims a poison arrow across the bed, cover the offending corner at bedtime. You can also cover the television screen when it is not used. Keep the bathroom door closed when you're sleeping. Hotel rooms are an excellent place to use aromatherapy because it really feels like you are claiming the space.

Sleeping Outside

Sleeping porches

Sleeping porches became popular at the beginning of the twentieth century. Of course, people in warm climates had frequently kept a bed on the back porch for use on hot summer nights. Sleeping porches gained popularity in the early 1900s because of the Arts and Crafts movement. They were often a feature (usually on the second floor) of Craftsman houses. They provided an opportunity to get plenty of fresh air while sleeping. Part of the Arts and Crafts philosophy was a return to simpler, more natural ways.

Fresh air while sleeping is certainly laudable, but the degree of openness on a porch is not conducive to deep rest. If you wish to use your sleeping porch try to make it feel a bit more enclosed. Open or screened sides should preferably have a solid half-wall up to waist height. Some tall potted plants along the open walls can also help to enclose and define a space. The head of the bed should be against a solid wall. Often the only solid wall is the one with the doorway into the house. This places the bed in a disempowered position, so a mirror should be positioned on the opposite "wall." That "wall" may consist of only a few support posts, so attach a mirror to one of them. A convex mirror may be the best option, or even gazing ball. See Empowered Positions, Chapter 3. If the bed cannot be placed against a solid wall, it must have a large, solid, headboard.

Camping

Some tents have structural support bars that are visible inside the tent. These are usually not a great concern in modern tents, which use tensile strength for their structure. There is no pressure *down* on the support bars as there is on structural beams in a building. If the support bars really do hold something *up* such as in old-fashioned pup tents, try to pin some fabric over the support bar. It never hurts to cover support bars in any tent, especially if you will be there for more than three nights. A tree that is directly outside a tent door should be at least six feet away.

Foam pads are preferred to air mattresses, because of the pressurized vibration of the air mattress. Who wants a vacation with pressure vibes! When tent camping, sleep with your head away from the door of the tent.

When sleeping in the great outdoors with no tent, you're going to get some great fresh air, but you're not likely to get great sleep. It's okay occasionally, such as when watching meteor showers, but not on a regular basis. Even something as simple as a mosquito net will allow the rest to be deeper.

Rooms for the Sick

If someone is bedridden, make sure there is green in the room. It is relaxing and represents healing. There should be adequate air circulation (preferably fresh air). A sick person appreciates peace and quiet. Bring fresh chi to them by touching or massaging them. Too many sick people only have contact with a remote control. Sick (and elderly) people should not sleep in the same room as very young children. Their vibes are quite different, and neither will get their best rest. If they must be in the same room, put a curtain or screen between the beds.

A view of nature from a sick person's window is highly recommended for its healing properties. Consider a birdfeeder.

Chapter 15

Adjacent Bathrooms

The worst building fad I've noticed is putting bathtubs and sinks right in the actual bedroom. This is truly horrible feng shui. It's usually in very expensive homes, and it's what I call having more dollars than sense. Keep the drains in the bathroom—don't ever bring them into the bedroom. The best solution is to call a plumber and take it out.

Laying down a bagua for a regular-sized bathroom is a losing proposition. The space is just too small to make effective statements for each of the nine areas. Instead, look at where the bathroom is within the bagua of the whole home. If the bathroom is in the Creativity area of the whole home, go for chrome and pastels. If it is in the Relationship area of the home, go for pinks, reds, yellows, and/or whites, and groupings of things. A bathroom in the Fortunate Blessings area should look royal—lots of purple, blue, gold, or red, and it should be ultra-neat and clean. Use the appropriate bagua colors, depending on where the bathroom is in the house. Bring in those colors with such things as towels, bathmats, shower curtain, soap dish, or soap squirter.

A bedroom should not be located above or below a bathroom. If that's the case see the solutions offered in the Kitchens section of Chapter 2, Location of the Bedroom. The bathroom is the "disturbance" that gets reflected away from the quiet bedroom.

Don't store food or items associated with food, such as napkins, in a bathroom.

Doors

When you're in the bedroom and you're just about to open the bathroom door, there should be a clear crystal over your head hanging from the ceiling bedroom ceiling. It symbolizes that the bedroom and bathroom energies don't mix and mingle. Instead, the two energies are dispersed. There should always be a solid (not louvered) door between the bedroom and the bathroom. It's a very good idea to put a full-length mirror on the bedroom side of the door, to symbolically *erase* the bathroom. It is best to keep the bathroom door closed most of the time and, without fail, the door should be kept closed at night when you are sleeping. That way the moist, body waste, "drain" vibration doesn't seep into the bedroom or the rest of the home. Consider a self-closing hinge on the door—they're easy to install. Sliding doors can be a hassle to open and close at night, but if that's what you've got, use them. This is a serious feng shui concern because the bathroom is the most problematic room and the bedroom is the most important room.

A large number of bedrooms either have a bathroom attached or share a wall with a bathroom. If the bathroom opens immediately into the bedroom there *must* be a door between the two rooms. If there is an en suite bathroom, with no door between the two rooms, add a door or curtains.

Sometimes an en suite bathroom has two entrances, one from each side of the bed. If that's the case, and it's possible to walk in one door and come out the other and continue going in a circle, it's called a whirlwind or racetrack. It symbolizes expending energy but getting nowhere. Hang a crystal or tiny wind chime from the ceiling someplace that would be over your head if you were walking in that circle. It can be in the bathroom or the bedroom. See Fig. 15.1. Another example is Fig. 7.6.

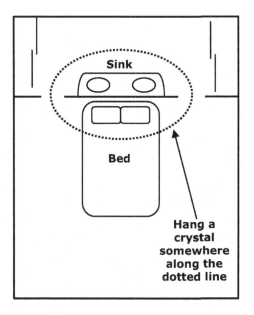

Whirlwind

Fig. 15.1

Occasionally the wall between the bedroom and the bathroom doesn't reach the ceiling. This sometimes happens when the rooms have slanted ceilings. If it's possible to extend the wall to the ceiling, do so. If that's not possible, then you need to create a symbolic barrier between the two rooms. On the top of the separating wall, put something like artificial plants, or hang a curtain in the upper space. A curtain is a better fix that the plants, but since the ceiling is usually slanted, it can require some creativity.

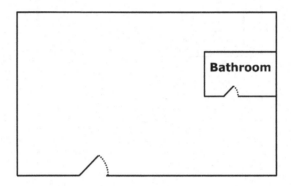

Front door and bathroom door same direction

Fig. 15.2

If the door going into the bathroom is in the same orientation as the front door, shown in Fig. 15.2, it is not auspicious. It weakens the energy of the front door and it also allows chi to find those drains too easily. Keep the bathroom door closed and hang a crystal outside the bathroom door.

If a bathroom door has hinges (and most do), I recommend hanging a very small wind chime from the ceiling so that the top of the door just barely touches the lowest point on the chime when the door opens about 5 inches. That will make a very tiny sound and lift the vibrations of the room. Because the sound is the first thing heard as you enter the bathroom, it has a more powerful effect. If there's any chance that the sound might disturb someone in bed, be sure it is a *very* faint sound.

**This wind chime is about three inches tall,
and the top of the bathroom door barely touches it.**

Some bathroom doors are as tall as the ceiling, so the above-mentioned wind chime remedy won't work. In that case, either attach a small L-bracket to the inside of the bathroom door (up high) and hang the tiny wind chime (so it doesn't knock against the door), or use a door harp. Door harps are available on eBay.

Drains

The reason the bathroom is the most problematic room in the house, according to feng shui, is largely because of the drains. Water symbolizes money, and a drain is where water leaves your home. A standard bathroom has at least three drains, often more. Each of those drains is an opportunity for chi to drain down and out of your life. To keep chi from draining away, keep the drains covered as much as possible. A drain is a "weakness" in the floor or wall of your home, because an otherwise solid surface now has a hole drilled in it. The seal of your home has been punctured.

If a drain of any kind is directly behind the head of the bed, a small mirror should be placed between the drain and the bed. The reflective side of the mirror should shine toward the drain, because its purpose is to symbolically reflect away the drain energy from the bed. The mirror can be placed under the sink or behind the bed in the bedroom.

If any of the bathroom fixtures drips, it symbolizes money being spent needlessly. Fixing it is usually (though not always) as simple as changing the rubber washer.

Sink Drains

Sink drains often have a built-in metal stopper that hides most of the actual drain hole. These are great, because all that you see is a tiny sliver of the drain hole. Also, the reflective stopper repels chi away from the drain. Don't let that stopper get grimy! It's quite easy to close the drains all the way.

If the sink is older, it probably doesn't have a built-in metal stopper. It can be inconvenient to keep moving the stopper every time the sink is used. These sinks benefit from having a hair-catching strainer, which reduces the size of the drain hole.

Put a circle of red string, ribbon, or tape around the drainpipe to symbolically cut off the drain energy. Make sure not to put it around the *incoming* water pipes, just the drainpipe, which is usually in the center. Say out loud, "I am cutting off the drain." or words to that effect. Also put a very heavy object (such as a twenty-five pound weight or very heavy rock) directly under the sink to ground the energy that's flowing away. In this case, you would say out loud, "This heavy object symbolizes that my good fortune is grounded and does not flow away" or words to that effect.

Tub and Shower Drains

Tub and shower drains should be kept as covered or closed as possible. In addition, keep the shower curtain or door pulled so the drain area isn't seen. If it must remain partly open for ventilation, the part that is seen should be away from the drain.

A very heavy object can also be used at the drain end of a claw-foot tub to represent grounding. The heavy object should be stable and unmoving, so don't use something that could actually roll like a bowling ball.

Toilet

The toilet is the most offensive drain in the home. This is partly because of what happens there, but mostly because of the drain hole's size. It is the largest drain hole in the home—judged by its size where it disappears from view. The toilet drain is so easy to hide—just keep the lid down when it's not in use. It is *much* more important to keep the toilet lid down than to keep sink and tub drains plugged. Develop the habit yourself, but do not harangue your guests. Close the lid before flushing. I use an inexpensive, self-closing lid at home and it changed my life!

There are two other ways to deal with chi draining away. Put a *very* large round rock on the floor directly behind the toilet. Large—because it is acting as a grounding object. Round—because it will need to be wiped clean occasionally. It's big, it's heavy, it ain't goin' anywhere. The rock should be too large to flush down the toilet. The ideal rock is so big that it takes two hands to carry it. This counters the flush and drain vibration of the toilet. If the bathroom has a ceramic tile floor, put felt on the bottom of the rock to avoid damaging the tile.

Snake Plant (Sansevieria) can be used effectively around the toilet or tub to counter the drain down vibrations. Its strong uprising form says "no" to the down-and-out vibrations very effectively. Place it in pots on the floor on each side of the toilet tank. Snug the pots right up against the wall, and as far under the tank as they can go without bending the leaves. If your tank is out from the wall a bit, you might even have leaves coming up from behind the tank. Don't have any of the leaves terribly close to the seat. A pot of Sansevieria can also be placed on top of the toilet tank or near any bathroom drain.

It is best if the toilet is not reflected in a mirror, because that symbolically doubles the number of toilets. It's fine if a toilet is reflected in a tiny mirror that is symbolically reflecting the drain energy back to the toilet, so that it doesn't adversely affect other parts of the building. Try never to place a bed below a toilet (or any drain) that is directly above in the building. Likewise, don't place a bed directly above a toilet that is on a lower floor of the building. If there is no choice and the bed is above a toilet, put a small mirror under the bed facing down toward the floor. It is symbolically reflecting the toilet energy back down. Or, if you have access to that bathroom, you could place the mirror on the bathroom ceiling directly reflecting down on the toilet. That's actually a good thing to do for any toilet, but I can't recommend it in a bathroom used by guests, because it can look like a camera lens, and make people *very* uncomfortable. If a bed has to be right below a toilet, put a small mirror on the ceiling of the bedroom with the reflective side facing up to the ceiling. It should be located exactly where the toilet is above it. The back of the mirror can be painted to match the ceiling color, so it won't be very noticed.

Do not keep a plunger in view next to the toilet. The plunger says "dysfunctional toilet." Store it away in a cabinet or closet. If the plunger is used frequently, call a plumber and deal with the more fundamental drainage problem.

Toilet paper should roll toward you, as if it were offering itself to you. You can't do this in a room that a cat has access to—if the cat has learned the entertaining trick of unrolling the whole roll.

Bidet

I suppose the reason bidets don't have lids is so that people won't confuse them with toilets. It's too bad that most of them don't have lids, but Toto makes a combination toilet and bidet, complete with lid. It's the only kind of bidet that I can recommend from a feng shui point of view. One client apologized that his wife used the bidet in her luxurious bathroom as a clothes hamper. I replied that it was about the best use I'd seen for a bidet, because you couldn't see the drain hole.

I met with a client and her architect, and saw a bidet on the plans for her huge new bathroom. I boldly asked her, "Are you going to use that?" She unhesitatingly said, "No." and I replied, "Don't put it in." The architect bristled, "A home of this stature *must* have a bidet." I looked her right in the eyes and said, "That's nonsense—if you're not going to use it, don't put it in. Go ahead and put the plumbing in for it, so that if you sell the house, you can add the bidet as a selling point. But don't have what looks like a big, extra open toilet in the bathroom while you're living here."

Moist Energy

A bathroom is a very yin room. It has no stove or oven to help balance the several areas of wetness (tub, shower, sinks, and toilet). If a bathroom is visually busy or complicated, this pushes the yin component off the scale, and the room becomes unbalanced and unhealthy. There are many ways to add yang to a bathroom, thereby making it more balanced energetically. It will then be healthier for the nearby rooms.

Add plants. Real or artificial plants are quite appropriate in a bathroom. Real plants appreciate the humidity and use it to build their plant bodies. They are physically converting the excess of water in that room into their leaves and stems. Pictures of plants are also good, because they are symbolically doing the same thing.

Have proper ventilation. The healthiest bathrooms are those that have at least one wall window that opens to the outside. (A *wall* window, not a skylight. Skylights are good, but not as good as a wall window in a bathroom.) Use the window regularly to ventilate and air out the bathroom. Nothing can beat fresh air. If there is no window, you have the beginning of an unhealthy bathroom. If mildew grows in your bathroom, deal with it. Mildew equals an unhealthy situation. The yin component is being pushed into the "rot realm." Clean it (all) out. (See *Speed Cleaning* in Recommended Reading.) Keep the ventilating fan on *all* the time that you are gone. You may choose not to keep the ventilating fan on very much when you are home because of the motor sound, but when you are leaving, turn the fan on. The ventilation will dry the bathroom (making it more yang) and mildew will not regrow (eliminating the excessively yin "rot" vibration).

Fresh air is best, and direct sunlight is ideal. It can totally eliminate a dank smell, which should not just be masked. Pleasant fragrance is appreciated in a bathroom, but it cannot replace fresh air. For most of humanity's history, bathrooms have been outbuildings, without influencing the main living space. Modern plumbing (a comparatively recent invention) allows bathrooms to be anywhere. If the bathroom is situated *with* an outside window, it retains some of that removed, outside connection, and doesn't influence the rooms around it as much.

Add red to represent Fire. The vibration of Fire is uprising and it lifts the drain vibe of the bathroom. It is usually more appropriate to represent Fire with color than with shape in the bathroom because angular objects can seem unfriendly in such a small room. Red does not have to be the main theme color, but it would be good if it could be there somewhere. It's fine to use plenty of red if that works in the decor. It's a relief to know that green can be used if red is completely inappropriate. Green represents Wood, which feeds Fire. Candles are good in bathrooms.

Keep it simple—almost to the point of austere. Don't use patterned wallpaper or a patterned shower curtain (unless the pattern has plant imagery). A bathroom can be elegant and feel wonderful by simply having color as the unifying theme. Avoid tchotchkes, knickknacks, and clutter of any kind in this room. It's usually best if the purely decorative objects are wall decoration—pictures, wall sculptures or wall pockets. Wall pocket is the technical name for a wall vase. They come in all sizes and styles. Look on eBay and you'll see many nice ones (as well as some tacky ones). Wall pockets look great with plants in them—either real or artificial. The plant is symbolically sucking up the wetness of the bathroom and balancing the energy.

Keep fabric to a minimum because it is a yin material. Use natural fabrics for towels, washcloths, and rugs, but avoid any other fabric use if possible. It's okay to use a fabric shower curtain, but it should dry quickly. Do not use a shower liner *and* a shower curtain. It's too much fabric and it's too fussy. If you can achieve window privacy without curtains, don't have them.

Don't use water imagery. It's fine for a bathroom to have a picture or two, but there should not be any water in the picture. Also don't decorate with seashells or images of fish, dolphins, or other water creatures. Those things say "water."

Electric lighting is Fire, and is therefore good in a bathroom. Bathroom light fixtures should be simple, not too fancy. "Fancy" is yin and should be avoided in bathrooms. Bathroom light bulbs are discussed in Chapter 8, Lighting.

It is considered disrespectful to have dragon imagery in a bathroom—likewise don't put religious imagery in bathrooms.

Chapter 16

Implementation of What You've Learned

Priorities for Feng Shui Changes

The first priority is to listen to your *intuition*. If certain feng shui changes are screaming to be done (and can be done quickly), then do them. Common sense goes hand-in-hand with intuition. Keep them alive in your life by acting on them.

The second priority is to *eliminate outside influences*. Use mirrors outside any window or door that has a foreboding object pointing at it. See Windows, Chapter 7.

The third priority is to *clean* thoroughly and well, including windows if they need it. Then continue to clean well on a regular basis. Make it easy on yourself by doing it the professional way, as taught in *Speed Cleaning*. (See Recommended Reading.) If you don't already have the habit of making your bed each morning, do so.

Once you've cleaned thoroughly, consider *painting* the walls or ceiling. If you've always had white bedroom walls, you'll be amazed at the positive change of adding a favorite color. You don't have to paint all the walls, and you can always paint over it if you don't like the new color or when you leave (if you're a renter). On my advice, one of my clients painted the far wall of her bedroom red. She used a very rich, sophisticated color between dark maroon and crimson. Her large wooden headboard was then placed against the center of the wall. The effect was stunning. When she was in bed, she saw the three white walls, but when she opened the door to come into her bedroom, there was the beautiful red. She said, "I realize how it affects chi energy because when I see it I am pulled into the room." Some feng shui teachers advise against blue walls in a relationship bedroom, because it is a cool color. It can symbolize a chilled relationship. Also be cautious if painting green in a relationship bedroom, because certain greens look cold. If it's a relationship bedroom and you want green walls, make sure it's a *warm* green.

Next, find out if there are any *missing areas* and bring them back with mirrors or other ways. See Chapter 10.

After that, *empower yourself* by making sure that you can see the door from the bed and/or desk. See Chapter 3.

Now is the time to deal with *clutter* if you haven't already. If you are awash in clutter, make time for organizing. Make it a priority. Clutter can stop everything. Even if your stuff seems well organized, if there's too much of it, you will be blocking your feng shui success. Please take this seriously and trim your possessions back to what is truly useful in your life right now. Also keep things you love, but do not use that as an excuse to keep everything! Once the decision has been made to get rid of an object, carry out the decision quickly. As mentioned in the section on Clutter in Chapter 7, start near the doorway and in the Fortunate Blessings corner.

Once clutter and too many possessions are gone, *apply the bagua*. If certain life areas are more important right now, emphasize them first. I generally recommend beginning with the Fortunate Blessings area, because it represents intention. Things that might be seen as "coincidences" can be the Universe responding to your "request" via the bagua.

Space Clearing

Space clearing is not a priority or even a necessity for everyone. However, if the bedroom has never had any type of vibrational cleansing, please consider it. This is especially important if someone has died in the room, or if it was once a relationship bedroom and the relationship has ended. (In that case, you should consider getting a different bed.)

Most of a space clearing is accomplished by thorough cleaning—ceiling to floor. Pay special attention to the carpet or rugs. Just as dirt can settle in there, so can old vibes. Here are a few tips for space clearing. Yes, you can do it yourself. In fact, it's probably more powerful if you do it yourself.

- Don't do it at night.
- Have every window open as fully as possible. Let the natural breezes do some of the work for you.
- Go around the entire inside perimeter of the bedroom, including closets. Go in a clockwise direction, which means turning to your left as soon as you have entered the room.
- Carry burning incense or a white sage smudge bundle (see Glossary).
- If possible, carry a pure-sounding bell, and ring it every few steps. If someone is assisting you, one can carry the incense, and the other can carry the bell.
- If no bell is readily available, use your hands and clap. Don't clap as if you were applauding. Do single, loud, sharp claps when you get to corners and doorways and any place that feels a little unusual—*any kind* of unusual. It is an extremely powerful, assertive thing to do. You are using your own hands to claim your rightful ownership of a space. Clap high and clap low. You cannot clap and hold incense at the same time, so if you are doing this alone, you will have to make two complete circuits. If you have time, go ahead and make a third circuit. You cannot overdo it and three is a very powerful number.
- Sing, chant, or speak aloud—whichever you are most comfortable with. The very ancient chant "Om" is always appropriate. Anything that you feel expresses your intention is appropriate. You could simply say, "Peace to this room," over and over. There are some instances when your voice should sound assertive and rather loud. If the room or home has a troubled history, or has an unsettled feel in any way, you should say things like, "Get out!" or "Scat!" like you really mean it. Say it as if you are shooing out an unwelcome cat.

- Be sure the smoke from the incense wafts high and low. Bring the incense near the floor and the ceiling, in every corner, including closets and cabinets. Open drawers and cabinet doors. Move the incense all around every object in the room, including under the bed. Do an ultra-thorough job. It may take a while, but you are not likely to be doing it very often.
- These are the good times to do a space clearing: when you first move in, on your birthday, and at the time of a new year (Chinese or Western or both). Also, a space clearing is very appropriate after any severe trauma in the room, such as loud arguments or thievery.

Any time a second-hand object is brought into your home, and especially into your bedroom, it is important to clear the old energy from the object. Waft white sage smoke *thoroughly* over and under and around the object while saying something like, "All old vibrations have to leave now." It's best to do it outside, during the day. If you can't do it outside, do it next to an open window.

Recommended Reading

I recommend that you support new and used bookstores in your area. I also shop on bookfinder.com, which widens my sources considerably. However, I use that plucky eBay to get the very best price for hard-to-find books. Be patient and they'll notify you when the item comes up for sale. If the eBay item is not a "Buy It Now" item, use an auction sniping service, such as JustSnipe. Don't shop too much, but do shop wisely.

Feng Shui

Feng Shui Demystified: Revised Edition by Clear Englebert

This book jumps right in to information on how to do feng shui effectively. It does not dwell on such things as the history of feng shui. The writing is concise and very understandable. When a problem is described, multiple solutions are always suggested. I realize that you can't just move if something is "wrong" about your home. There is always a way to fix a bad situation (no matter how ornery) and in a way that will fit with your decor. I've tried to be especially sensitive to renters, who have even less control over their abode than home owners. The revised edition is the ninth anniversary edition and a much more powerful book than the earlier edition.

Feng Shui for Hawaii by Clear Englebert

This is my most beautiful book, and it makes a great gift. It's in full color at a low price, and the principles apply absolutely anywhere. It just hasn't received wide distribution because the word Hawaii is in the title. Even though it doesn't cover the bagua, I can easily say this is my best book. The publisher, Watermark Publishing, sometimes has this book marked down in price on their website, bookshawaii.net.

"This is the most user friendly book on Feng Shui I have ever read. I bought it while living in Hawaii and I am continuing to use it while in Northern California. The basic information applies in any location and this book is filled with beautiful photographs, especially helpful for those of us who learn best and most quickly visually. I was fortunate to hear Clear Englebert speak while I was in Hawaii and he writes in the same engaging and solution-oriented manner. This is the first time I have felt both inspired and confident to make the necessary changes without feeling I need to make a significant time or financial investment first." Kathleen Casey, Sonoma, California

Feng Shui House Book by Gina Lazenby

Plenty of feng shui books with color photographs have been (and continue to be) published. They are usually pricey, and often not worth the money. This book is well worth the price. The pictures are a feng shui education. It stands head and shoulders above most other feng shui books with color photography, because of Lazenby's extensive commentary. She does what almost no other author does—she comments on *everything* in the picture. It's frustratingly common to find feng shui books illustrated with pictures full of poison-arrow beams, et cetera, and the author's only comment is on the color of the couch. This is such a disservice because readers might think that the beams (or dark ceiling fan, for example) are somehow okay because nothing is said to the contrary. Lazenby does the opposite. She goes the extra mile by even pointing out what else could be done to improve the situation. Her writing is power-packed. She can say in one sentence what some authors require a paragraph for. Even the structure of the chapters is a breath of fresh air.

There is a very condensed version of this book, called *Simple Feng Shui* by Gina Lazenby. The print is sometimes quite small, but it is considerably cheaper.

Feng Shui and Health by Nancy SantoPietro

This is one of the best feng shui books, a true masterpiece. The section on bedrooms is quite substantial. The drawings are very detailed and packed with commentary. SantoPietro is also the author of *Feng Shui: Harmony by Design*. Anything she writes is a must-read to understand feng shui well.

Modern Book of Feng Shui by Steven Post

There is an abundance of information in this book by the first American teacher of feng shui. If you are looking for an excuse to keep mirrors in the bedroom, read page 68 and breathe easy. He includes a well-illustrated section on blessings and rituals and full instructions for using a bagua based on the entrance.

Move Your Stuff, Change Your Life by Karen Rauch Carter

This book conveys serious life-changing information in a light-hearted way. Carter's jovial tone keeps you happily turning pages all the way to the end. The book contains a hefty chapter for each area of the bagua. These nine chapters contain what you need to know about feng shui in general, such as poison arrows and elemental cycles. What isn't covered there is dealt with in the final two chapters. The author is refreshingly forthright, and so are the drawings.

Practical Feng Shui by Simon Brown

This is one of the finest feng shui books ever written. All aspect of Compass feng shui are explained and illustrated. He explains more stuff, more understandably, than most other authors. The charts and illustrations are among the best I've seen. A beginner will not get lost or bogged down, and the more advanced feng shui reader will appreciate how much is packed into this powerful book. If you practice Compass Feng Shui (which I don't) *Practical Feng Shui* will probably be one of your most referred-to feng shui books.

Western Guide to Feng Shui by Terah Kathryn Collins

The text is complete and well supplemented with truly excellent graphics. Her writing is lucid, making it very accessible for beginners. The chapters on individual guas include numerous suggestions for affirmations. There is also an audio set available from the same publisher.

Wind and Water: Your Personal Feng Shui Journey by Carol Hyder

The style of this book is somewhat unique for a feng shui book. No section is more than one page long, and each is chock full of introspective knowledge. It is as if you are reading aphorisms or daily reminders. Her approach is powerful and will allow the reader to understand more deeply what feng shui changes are all about. It is also available on audio.

Bedrooms for Youth

The Peaceful Nursery by Carlin and Forbes

The subtitle is *Preparing a Home for Your Baby with Feng Shui*, and it's incredibly detailed, even having bagua tips for the nursery. The thoroughness of this book is quite amazing.

Teen Feng Shui by Susan Levitt

I've seen several books on this subject, but Levitt's is the best. Its format is user-friendly, the information is exactly right, and the cures are doable. Levitt is the author of *Taoist Feng Shui* and *Taoist Astrology*. Everything she writes is touched with brilliance.

Family Bed by Tine Thevenin

Beds where young children sleep with their parents are common in the world. There are now several books out on this subject (including one on how to get kids to sleep in their own beds), but this is the original and classic book on the subject.

Everyday Blessings: The Inner Work of Mindful Parenting by Kabat-Zinn

This book is by a very caring pair of parents. If you need any prodding to make your children have less screen-viewing time, read their chapter Media Madness. It profoundly asks the right questions to motivate you.

Cleaning, Maintenance and Organizing

Speed Cleaning by Jeff Campbell

Cleaning is as essential to feng shui as breathing is to life. This is by far the best book on cleaning ever published. It should be taught in schools, because sooner or later everybody has got to do some cleaning—may as well be smart about it. As in feng shui, this book isn't afraid to state the obvious. Some rules are shockingly simple, as in, "Work from top to bottom," "If it isn't dirty, don't clean it," "Pay attention," "Use both hands," "If there is more than one of you, work as a team," but when applied together, they make for fast, excellent cleaning. As he says, "It's worth it." A clean home is your best ticket to feng shui success.

Clutter Control by Jeff Campbell

One of the things I like best about Jeff Campbell's books is that he lays down the rules early on:

- *Use it or lose it.* The exact words that you will hear from many a feng shui teacher.
- *Use a file cabinet.* He makes a big case for hanging files and I agree completely.
- *Items displayed in the house have to pass a test.* "After all, you only have so much space. The items taking up that space should justify themselves. It's not a complicated test. They just have to have a valid reason for being there."
- *Label things.* Including (but not limited to) all storage boxes.

The second chapter, "The Psychology of Clutter," is quite powerful. Here Campbell tackles the three most common excuses used by packrats. 1) "I might need it someday." 2) "They don't make them like this any more." 3) "It reminds me of someone I love or someplace I've been." One-by-one he offers rebuttals to those rationalizations. The bulk of the book is devoted to a huge alphabetical list of places to de-clutter (cupboards, closets . . .)

and particular things (paper, photographs, keys . . .) This is an extremely useful book. When your home is less cluttered, it will not only be easier to clean—it will support you in reaching your goals (rather than working against you)!

All Jeff Campbell's books are great and they are available through his company, The Clean Team, www.thecleanteam. com, 800-717-2532.

Getting Organized by Stephanie Winston (audio)

Organizing is basic to feng shui, because it is essential to a well-functioning life—but saying it and doing it are two very different things! For some people, to be organized is a major lifestyle challenge. The outcome can seem attractive, but getting from here to there can be daunting. The good news is that the audio version of *Getting Organized* can seep into you by osmosis. Keep listening to it until you are doing it—all of it. Stephanie Winston does cover all of it—every aspect of being organized. Her voice carries a confidence that helps get you there. The best advice I can give anyone who wants to be better organized is to listen to Stephanie Winston. I've read scores of organizing books, and this one stands high—especially the audio version.

Getting Things Done by David Allen

Feng shui is about changing lives and this book changed my life. I just thought I was organized and productive before I read it. The person who recommended the book to me is someone I trust greatly, so I hopped right on it when I heard about it. Allen's system is quite brilliant and useful in everyone's life, even if you're not a businessperson. Learn some new organizing habits and allow your life to unfold in a magnificent way—I kid you not! I now have the audio version as well. This stuff should be taught to every teenager—how else are they going to know?

Saving Stuff by Don Williams and Louisa Jaggar

Williams is the Senior Conservator at the Smithsonian, which has to preserve all kinds of stuff. Every kind of thing you can imagine is expertly covered. If you've got stuff, this book completely educates you on how to keep it well. If you don't have stuff, you don't need this book.

Interiors

The Bed by Alecia Beldegreen

This is mostly a book of large romantic color pictures of beds, bed details, and bedrooms (apparently European), and it's got some great ideas for bed canopies. It also has some fascinating information on the different natural materials that sheets are made of. Personally I use flat cotton in the summer and cotton flannel in the winter and I've never considered thread count.

The Healthy House Book by Gina Lazenby

There's a section on the bedroom and a section on sleeping. Lazenby chooses words and images with great care. She is always worth reading.

Healing Environments by Carol Venolia

There's much to learn from this very quotable book. From page 59 comes this gem of knowledge: "Red and blue are the two color 'poles,' in terms of human response. Red increases blood pressure, respiration rate, heartbeat, muscle activity, eyeblinks, and brain waves, while blue lowers all of these measures. Green or yellow-green produces a neutral response." I would quote the entire next paragraph, but in fairness to the author, get the book and read the next paragraph on "centrifugal" and "centripetal" colors. It's fascinating! Page 143 has this about sleep conditions: "In the ideal situation, the skin is well insulated and the air is slightly cool. The recommended air temperature is 60° to 65° F. If blankets weigh more than a total of seven pounds, their weight will also disturb sleep." Nice information throughout the book.

Lighting Style by Kevin McCloud

I have owned three bookstores and have seen a multitude of books on lighting. I think *Lighting Style* is the best, because McCloud teaches and you *learn*. There is a wealth of information presented with brilliant illustrations. He shows the same room with different kinds of lighting and you really see the effects. I especially appreciated the section at the end explaining the different kinds of light bulbs. This book is of enduring value.

Straight Talk on Decorating by Lynette Jennings

This is the all-round best book on decorating that I've seen. Page 126 and on will tell you *everything* you need to know to use interesting colors harmoniously in your bedroom and in your home. Interior colors can clash and thereby bring a vibe of disharmony to the room. With Jennings' advice, your home will hum.

Fabric

New Upholstery by Diane Wallis

If you've got a headboard that is open (bars or slats) and would like it to look more solid, this book has two stylish projects with step-by-step instructions. These are the least intimidating "upholstery" projects imaginable. They're basically just slipcovers that fit over the existing headboard. Fabric is a great way to bring the right color into a room. Do so harmoniously with the advice from *New Upholstery.*

Winning Windows by Judy Sheridan

There are many fine books available on window treatments. *Winning Windows* is one of them. The book is composed of case studies, complete with drawings and photographs. Most importantly Sheridan explains the thinking that preceded the design, and then produced it. This truly empowers readers with the necessary knowledge to approach their own window challenges. Sheridan is excellent at showing how details can complete a look. Many of the windows will seem overly fussy to some people. But the vast amount of fabric involved is quite perfect for bedrooms because of its yin quality. Not all the window treatments are overblown. Some are refreshingly simple, such as Roman shades or balloon shades.

Window Style by Mary Linton

This book has window treatments that are less traditional than those in the previous book. Linton relies on colors and textures for a clean, unfussy look. The fabric shutter on page 96 is a model of minimalist simplicity. A fabric banner hangs from a hinged brass curtain rod so that it can swing back fully from the window and let maximum light shine in. The assembly instructions for the innovative designs are well thought out and illustrated. This book opens your vocabulary and your mind to the many possibilities in simple window treatment. There's even a great section on combinations, such as curtains and shades—which are both practical and lovely. Combinations are the key to restful bedroom window treatments.

Related Topics

Dream Book by Betty Bethards

Inner Light Foundation, Petaluma, California, 707-765-2200, innerlight.org

This is the best dream dictionary ever published—and there is ample information on how to decode a dream. There is a separate audio, *Dreams*, which is also the best of its kind. Learning to tap accurately into what our dreams are telling us is one of the most powerful things we can do. The book and the audio are a great combination.

Insomnia: 50 Essential Things to Do by Theresa DiGeronimo

I'm a light sleeper, and therefore I know a peaceful sleep situation when I see one. Sometimes, however, it's not just the physical circumstances of the room that are keeping a person form getting good sleep. If solid sleep eludes you, read this book and you're very likely to find a solution. It's quite thorough.

Beyond Antibiotics: 50 (or so) Ways to Boost Immunity and Avoid Antibiotics by Schmidt, Smith, and Sehnert

I'm including this book because pages146 and 147 have a marvelous list of 11 "Rules for Better Sleep Hygiene."

Disconnect: The Truth About Cell Phone Radiation, What the Industry Has Done to Hide It, and How to Protect Your Family by Devra Davis

Some people actually sleep with cell phones under their pillows! If you don't believe that cell phones and other devices that emit electromagnetic radiation can cause brain tumors and other serious health problems, that's because the cell phone industry has worked hard to counter independent studies that show that they do. The harm can take decades to show up, and that means when you see people going around with a cell phones glued to their ears, what you're seeing is an epidemic in slow motion. This book is easy to read and very eye-opening.

The Body Electric: Electromagnetics and the Foundations of Life by Robert Becker and Gary Seldon

This book is much more technical than the previous book in this list, but if you, or someone you know, needs more convincing, this is the book to do it. Becker was a physician and researcher who had his funding cut off because the powers-that-be didn't like the honest results of his studies.

Change Your Handwriting, Change Your Life by Vimala Rodgers

This book is about the energy of handwriting. Just as you can change your life by moving your stuff around in feng shui, you can also change your life by changing how you form the letters of the words that you write. It's the feng shui of handwriting and it's very common-sense and powerful.

Sources

Gaussmeters

Alphalab, 800-658-7030, www.trifield.com
They sell gaussmeters for measuring EMFs—electromagnetic fields. I've owned their Trifield meter for years. It's relatively expensive, but I've seen other brands on Amazon for as little as $30. Electromagnetic radiation is invisible but quite real and measurable. More people should own gaussmeters, so that they can show friends, family, and coworkers what they are being exposed to.

Tiny Wind chimes

Karizma, 415-861-4515, Karizma1@att.net
An excellent source for tiny wind chimes.

Bagua Mirrors

If there's not a Chinatown or Chinese dry goods store in your area, try eBay for a good selection and a wide range of prices. See Photo 7.8.

Seal-of-Solomon Mirrors

Lavender Moon Gallery, 808-324-7708, lavendermoongallery.com
The mirrors are surrounded by stained glass lotus frames in a choice of colors—very beautiful. See Photo 7.8.

Sage

Juniper Ridge, 800-205-9499, www.juniperridge.com
A source of excellent sage incense for clearing.

Crystals

Xinacat Prisms and Crystal Jewelry, http://stores.shop.ebay.
com/XinaCat-Prisms-and-Crystal-Jewelry
An eBay store with an excellent selection of crystals at decent
prices. A good place to get the best clear octagonal crystals.

Magnetic sleep pad

MAGNETICo, Calgary, Alberta, Canada 800-265-1119 (outside
of North America call 1-403-730-0883), magneticosleep.com.

Bullnose Corner

Specifically, the Shotgun High Impact Corner Guard, which
is near the bottom of this webpage: www.lobbysolutions.com/
guards.html

Glossary

Bullnose Corners

These are premolded drywall beads that form a radius instead of making a sharp right angle. They are applied after the Sheetrock but before mudding. They can also be installed at any time. See the previous section, Sources, or check the telephone directory under drywall supplies.

Chi

Pronounced chee. The basic energy of the Universe.

Crystals

Clear, faceted crystals made of lead glass or natural mineral represent dispersing energy, because they can disperse clear light into colors. Octagonal shapes are best in windows and the disco-ball shape is good everywhere else.

Elements

There are five elements according to Taoism: Water, Wood, Fire, Earth, and Metal. (The word Element here has nothing to do with the Periodic Table of Elements of Western science.) In Taoism it refers to archetypal energy. Everything in the Universe is considered to be an expression of one of the Elements.

Gaussmeter

A device that measures magnetism, which is measured in gauss. See Sources.

Gua or Guas

The Chinese name for any of the nine bagua areas. Guas is the plural. See Chapter 9.

I Ching

The *I Ching* is an ancient Chinese oracle, considered by many to be the oldest book in the world.

Magnetic Sleep Pad

A pad with magnets in it, which usually goes under the mattress, providing an even, negative, magnetic field for your body. There are several reputable manufacturers. See Sources.

Poison Arrow

This (malevolent) chi energy has various names: sha chi, or shar. It is chi energy that has encountered something in the environment to cause it to speed up or get irritated. See Poison Arrows, Chapter 6.

Sage Smudge Stick

This is sometimes called a sage wand. It is a tightly bound bundle of dried sage sticks and leaves. Usually wild sage is used. It is lit at the tip end, and then the flame is extinguished (usually by waving it rapidly rather than by using one's breath). It continues to smolder, and makes a lot of smoke. You'll probably want to temporarily disable the smoke alarm in the room before using it. You have to fan it or blow on it occasionally to keep it smoldering. Sage smudging is a Native American technique. It's messier than plain incense because it drops bits of black ash around the room. It is a powerful tool for eliminating negative vibrations, but use it with an awareness of fire safety. (I wouldn't dream of doing it over white carpet.) One incense company makes a sage incense of superior quality—Juniper Ridge, under Sage in Sources.

Silver Tip Light Bulb

A light bulb that looks as if the top of the rounded part was dipped in silver paint. It provides a subdued light, and directs the flow of the energy back toward the wall or ceiling. Fig. 2.5 in Chapter 2 has a drawing of a silver tip bulb turned on.

Trigram

The basic unit of a trigram is a line, either solid (yang) or with an opening in the middle (yin). The yin line is sometimes called a broken like, because it doesn't continue all the way across. When combined in units of three lines, there are only eight possible combinations. They are listed on the Chart of Bagua Areas in Chapter 9 with their meanings.

Uplight

Any light fixture that directs the light upwards. It is used to symbolically push away energy that is above you. Examples of uplights are torchieres, wall sconces, and spotlights aimed up.

Wind Catcher

A wind catcher is any kind of silent decorative object that hangs outside and moves in the wind. They are especially useful in situations where the sound of a wind chime would be annoying. Some wind catchers are simply colorful threads that dangle.

Index

About the Author

Clear Englebert is a long-time feng shui consultant and teacher and an internationally acclaimed writer on feng shui. His first book, Feng Shui Demystified, was originally published in 2000 by The Crossing Press and reissued in a revised edition by iUniverse in 2010. He is also the author of two beautiful feng shui books with full color photographs throughout—Feng Shui for Hawaii and Feng Shui for Hawaii Gardens—both from Watermark Publishing. His books are available in four languages. He lives in Kona, Hawaii, and maintains the website fungshway.com.